EASY DUTCH PHRASE BOOK

Over 1500 Common Phrases
For Everyday Use And Travel

www.LingoMastery.com

ISBN: 978-1-951949-38-9

Copyright © 2021 by Lingo Mastery

ALL RIGHTS RESERVED

Free Book Reveals the 6-Step Blueprint That Took Students **from Language Learners to Fluent in 3 Months**

- **6 Unbelievable Hacks** that will accelerate your learning curve

- **Mind Training:** why memorizing vocabulary is easy

- **One Hack to Rule Them All:** This <u>secret nugget</u> will blow you away...

Head over to **LingoMastery.com/hacks**
and claim your free book now!

CONTENTS

INTRODUCTION

The Dutch language is a West Germanic language, which is closely related to the English language. Still, it has a complex grammar, and is full of tongue-twisting words filled with unique pronunciation of certain consonants. However, with our book, learning the basics of the Dutch language will be easier than you thought it would be. Experience with other foreign languages is definitely beneficial in the process, especially if you can speak German, but do not worry if you have none – many Dutch words are derived from English, which will be of great help to you! Dutch also uses the Latin alphabet, and since you are already familiar with its letters, you don't have to worry about having to master an entirely new alphabet.

Successful acquisition of a foreign language is based on making connections in your brain that help you memorize things, and then putting them in context when you need them most. Context is everything when it comes to learning a language, which is why most of the teaching practices present new vocabulary in thematic groups – here we will do just the same! Using this book, we will learn how to navigate the plethora of situations that travelers are likely to find themselves in – all those real situations that a tourist will experience.

So, how can Dutch (contrary to popular belief) be easy to learn? The main reason is that once you have become familiar with its pronunciation and spelling rules, which can admittedly take some time, it becomes reasonably easy to read and speak no matter what words you come across. Practice makes perfect, but be aware that you might need to spend more time working on your Dutch than you would when studying other languages.

There might be doubts crossing your mind right now. You are probably wondering if you will have to spend hours memorizing numerous rules and exceptions. The truth is – yes, there are plenty of rules to follow. But it is not as complicated as it sounds. Also, orthography will come to your rescue! *What kind of sorcery is this...,* you may ask? It is a set group of rules (and exceptions to such) for writing a language and it can be extremely helpful. It means writing in Dutch won't be the case of guessing which letters to use to write down a word, which can often be the case in English, but rather following fairly fixed conventions. You just need to be aware that it might take a while to memorize all the rules and exceptions, but after a while, you will also develop a natural feel for the language.

Let's start with the easy stuff. How exactly does one learn to read Dutch perfectly? Once you have found out how to pronounce each letter and group of letters, you will be able to fool many, making an impression of being fluent in the language. Do you want to give it a go?

Pronunciation of Dutch vowels

There are 5 basic vowels in Dutch: A, E, I, O, U

The vowel A

In Dutch, all vowels can be either short or long. The long 'a' is pronounced like 'a' in the English word father. A single 'a' is often short, pronounced like the 'a' in 'car', but even shorter, except for when it is not followed by another consonant or at the end of a word. In that case, you pronounce it just like the 'a' in 'father'.

Every time you see an 'a' in a Dutch word, you can think about the 'a' in 'alarm'; both of them sound like the short pronunciation of the Dutch 'a'. To make it even easier, the word for 'alarm' is the same in Dutch. Just like the English word, the accent is placed on the second syllable (al-ARM).

Notice how we capitalize the syllables that are stressed – this is a very important piece of information, which will allow you to pronounce words correctly from the very beginning.

Water (water), *VAH-ter*
// the 'a' in this word is a long vowel. Remember to use the 'a' sound in the English 'alarm'.

mama (mum), *MAH-mah*
// these two words sound similar but not the same – the 'u' in English 'mum' leaves your lips close together, the 'a' in Dutch makes you open them wide, as in 'car'. Both vowels in this word are short.

Anekdote (anecdote) *ah-nek-DOH-tuh*
// Make sure to pronounce each letter. In Dutch, unlike in French, every letter, even the one standing at the very end of the word, must be pronounced. The 'a' in this word is short.

The vowel E

Just like the letter 'a', the pronunciation of the letter 'e' changes depending on the word. The vowel can be either short or long. The short 'e' is often pronounced like the 'e' in the English word 'test'. The long 'e' is pronounced like the 'a' in the English word 'male'. In other instances, the Dutch 'e' can be pronounced like 'uh', as in the Dutch article 'Een', which is pronounced as 'uhn'.

element (element) *ey-luh-MENT*
// the word looks exactly the same, but in Dutch the stress falls on the last syllable, while in English, on the first one. The first 'e' is long, the middle 'e' is pronounced as 'uh' and the last 'e' is short.

Stem (voice) *STEM*
// simply add the Dutch short 'e' sound that you have just learned between 'st' and 'm', it couldn't be easier!

The vowel I

Again, there are two ways to pronounce the Dutch 'I': short and long. The long 'I' sounds just like the English 'ee' as in 'cheese' or 'need'. The short 'I' sounds like the 'I' in the English word 'wit' or 'sit'.

Internet (Internet) *IN-tuhr-net*
// written the same as in English and also sounds the same.

gratis (free) *GRAH-tis*
// the 'I' is pronounced short, like the 'I' in 'sit'.

Bizar (bizarre) bi-ZAHR
// these words look and sound very similar. However, the 'I' is pronounced more clearly than you would in English. Remember to pronounce the 'I' like you would in 'cheese'.

The vowel O

The long pronunciation of the Dutch 'o' is similar to the 'o' in the English word 'go'. The short pronunciation of 'o' sounds like the first 'o' in the English word 'hollow'.

kopen (buy) *KOH-puhn*
// the 'o' in this word is pronounced long, like the 'o' in the English word 'go'. The stress falls on the first syllable.

rond (round) *ROHND*
// this 'o' is pronounced short, like the first 'o' in 'hollow'.

over (about) *OH-fuhr*
// can you see how easy the Dutch language can be? Although the definition is different, the pronunciation of the word is almost exactly the same as in English. The only difference is the letter 'r', which is a guttural sound instead of a rolled sound like in English.

The vowel U

Just like all the other vowels, there is a short and long pronunciation for 'u'. The short pronunciation sounds like 'uh', similar to the 'a' in the English word 'alive'. There is no English equivalent to the long pronunciation of 'u', but it sounds a lot like the English pronunciation of 'ew', but with your lips rounded.

Julia (Julia, female name) *YOO-lee-ah*
// in Dutch, this name sounds quite similar to the English pronunciation, although the 'U' is pronounced shorter. Also, the J is not pronounced like 'dj', but softer like the 'y' in 'yes'.

stuk (piece) *STUHK*
// the 'u' is pronounced short, like the English pronunciation of 'Uh'.

Nu (now) noo
// The 'u' is pronounced similar to the double 'o' in English, for example in the word 'too'.

We know that all this might be confusing at first, and it will take some time for you to get your head around Dutch pronunciation. Dutch words can also look intimidating in the beginning. You will see more consonants than you could (and would ever want to) pronounce at once. But don't worry! Keep reading and by using our little tricks to make reading in Dutch easier, you will see that everything is pronounceable!

Dutch consonants

Similarities between consonants in Dutch and English

Let's start with the good news. Most Dutch consonants are similar in pronunciation to the English ones! These are: b, c, d, f, h, k, l, m, n, p, q, s, t, x, y, z.

There are a few important things to remember. In Dutch, the 'd' is often pronounced the same, although it is sometimes pronounced like 't', often when it is at the end of a word. The 'w' is pronounced with relaxed lips, instead of rounded lips like in English. Some consonants, like 'r' and 'g' are pronounced like a guttural sound. This might take some getting used to.

Dutch consonants that sound different than in English

These consonants are spelled in the same way as the English ones, but their pronunciation is different. This is the case with the following consonants:

Letter g

Let's start with the most difficult, and most infamous, Dutch consonant. The Dutch 'g' is a very distinctive sound, which can be hard to get used to at first. There is no similar sound in the English language. The 'g' is pronounced somewhat like a guttural 'h' sound, made at the back of your mouth, as if you are clearing your throat. Try listening to some audio recordings and imitate the sound. It might feel strange at first, but do not worry, you will get used to it! (Since there is no equivalent in English, there isn't an equivalent phonetic way to depict it either, and in this book we're just using the letter 'g'. However, please remember it's never pronounced like an English 'g'.)

> God (god) GOHT
> // these words are spelled the same but pronounced completely different. Remember to pronounce the 'g' as a guttural sound, as if you are clearing your throat. Also, remember the 'o' is a short vowel here, like the first 'o' in 'hollow'. The 'd' is pronounced like a 't'.
>
> Graag (gladly) GRAHG

// this is a difficult one. Start with the voiceless, guttural 'g' sound in the back of your mouth and continue to 'roll' the sound forward to the middle of your mouth towards an 'r'. Add a long 'a' and end with another guttural 'g'. This might take some practice.

Begin (begin) buh-GIN
// again, this word looks the same as in English, but is pronounced different. The stress falls on the last syllable, just like it would in English. In English, the 'e' is pronounced like an 'I', but in Dutch it sounds more like an 'uh'. Remember the guttural 'g', like you are clearing your throat, and put it all together.

Letter j

The Dutch 'j' is pronounced like the English 'y' in 'yes', or 'yellow'. This one is much easier than the 'g', although it may cause some confusion in the beginning. Let's look at some more complicated examples now.

Jarig (having one's birthday) YAH-rig
// the 'j' is pronounced like the 'y' in 'yes'. The 'a' in this word is a long vowel, like in 'alarm'. The 'r' is a rolling sound, at the back of the mouth, and remember to make the guttural 'g' sound. It might look intimidating but give it some practice!

Jongen (boy) YOHNG-uhn
// start with the 'j', pronounced like the English 'y'. Continue with a short 'o', like the first 'o' in the English word 'hollow'. The 'ng' sound is the same as in English, and the 'e' is pronounced like 'uh'.

Oranje (orange) oh-RAHN-yuh
// These words look similar and have the same meaning. In Dutch, the stress falls on the second syllable, instead of the first syllable like the English word for 'orange'. Start with a long 'o' as in 'go', continue with a rolling 'r' and a short 'a'. The combination of the letters 'n and j' might take some getting used to, but you just need to remember to clearly pronounce both sounds. The 'n' is pronounced the same as in English and remember to pronounce the 'j' like the 'y' in 'yes'.

Letter r

Th letter 'r' is also quite different from the English 'r'. There are two ways to pronounce the 'r' in Dutch, depending on its place in a word. At the beginning of a word, or before a vowel, the Dutch 'r' is a much harder sound than the English 'r'. It is more guttural, whereas the English 'r' is a soft, rolling sound. This 'r' is formed in the back of the mouth. Try listening to some recordings to compare the Dutch and English 'r' to get used to this sound. At the end of a word, the Dutch 'r' sounds similar to the English 'r'.

Rood (red) ROHT
// being at the beginning of the word, this 'r' is pronounced like a guttural sound. Remember the Dutch 'g', but make the sound more rolling. The 'o' is a long vowel, and the 'd' is pronounced like a 't'.

Radar (radar) RAH-dahr
// These words are spelled the same but pronounced different. The first 'r' is pronounced like a guttural sound, and the second 'r' is pronounced the same as the English 'r'. Instead of pronouncing the first 'a' as an 'e', it is pronounced like the long 'a' (as in father). The second 'a' is pronounced like a short 'a', which sounds similar to the English pronunciation in this word.

Ster (star) STER
// Again, these words look quite similar. The 'st' sound is the same as in English, and the 'e' is pronounced short, like in 'test'. Being at the end of the word, you can pronounce the 'r' the same as you would in English, although a bit less rolling and formed in the back of the mouth.

Letter v

The Dutch letter 'v' is often pronounced the same as the English 'v', although it is sometimes closer to an 'f'. Let's look at some examples.

Vader (father) FAH-duhr
// these words are quite similar, and their pronunciation is also close. However, keep in mind some important differences. The 'v' is pronounced the same as the 'f' in father. Open your mouth a little wider as you say the 'a'. The 'd' is pronounced like a regular 'd', and you finish the word just like you would in English ('er').

Verkeer (traffic) fuhr-KEYR
// just like the previous example, the 'v' sounds like an 'f'. The first 'e' is a short vowel, and the 'r' is pronounced like the English 'r', although a bit less rolling. Whenever you see a combination of two of the same vowels, this is always pronounced as a long vowel. The 'r' at the end of the word is pronounced like the Dutch guttural 'r'.

Levend (alive) LEY-fuhnd
// the 'v' is pronounced more like the English 'v' than the 'f'. The sound is a bit softer than in the previous examples, because it is in the middle of a word, instead of at the beginning. The first 'e' is a long vowel, which sounds similar to the English 'a' in 'came'. The 'd' is at the end of the word, which means it is pronounced like a 't'.

Letter w

The Dutch letter 'w' is pronounced with relaxed lips, instead of rounded like the English 'w'. Sometimes it sounds more like a 'v', like in 'vacation', but without the clear puff of air. This is pretty straightforward when 'w' stands alone (or is placed between vowels) but gets a little tricky when joined by other consonants. Then, it becomes almost like an 'f' sound. However, in an ideal world, where everyone cares about pronouncing everything exactly how it should be pronounced, it should remain as close to the 'v' sound as possible. You can practice with the examples below:

Wonen (to live) VOH-nuhn
// remember to stay close to the 'v' sound, but without the puff of air. The 'o' is a long vowel, and the 'e' sounds like 'uh'.

Dwaas (fool) DVAHS
// start with a soft sounding 'd' and try to stick to the 'v' sound as much as you can. Remember to hold back the urge to round your lips, as you would with an English 'w'.

Pronunciation of Dutch diphthongs

We are almost at the end of the many surprises that the Dutch pronunciation offers. There are just a few of them left so hold on tight.

CH

In Dutch, the combination of the vowels 'c' and 'h' sounds the same as the Dutch 'g'. It is never pronounced like the 'ch' in the English word 'chair'. Remember to imitate the sound of clearing your throat.

Chaos (chaos) GAH-ohs
// Even though these words are spelled the same, they sound very different. Remember to start with the guttural 'g' sound and pronounce the 'a' like the short vowel, instead of like an 'e' as you would in English.

Lachen (to smile) LAHG-uhn
// the 'a' is a short vowel in this word; remember to pronounce the 'ch' like the guttural 'g'. The 'e' is pronounced like 'uh'.

Schoenen (shoes) SGOO-nuhn
// the 'ch' is pronounced the same as the examples above but preceded by an 's'. The 'oe' is pronounced the same as you would in the English word 'shoes'.

NG

In Dutch, the combination of the letters 'n' and 'g' sounds the same as the 'ng' in the English word 'hang' or 'long'. It is never pronounced like the 'ng' n the English word 'danger'. Let's see some examples.

Lang (long) LAHNG
// these words look and sound quite similar. The only difference is the vowel 'a', which is a short vowel.

Zingen (to sing) ZING-uhn
// remember to pronounce the 'ng' like the 'ng' in the English word 'hang'. The 'I' is a short vowel, and the 'e' sounds like 'uh'.

OE

This vowel combination sounds the same as the 'oo' in the English word 'choose'.

Groen (green) GROON
// pronounce the 'oe' as the 'oo' in the English word 'choose'. Remember the gutteral 'g' and 'r' sounds; it might take some practice to get this combination down.

Snoep (candy) SNOOP

// remember to pronounce the 'oe' like the 'oo' in 'choose'. The combination of the consonants 's' and 'n' is pretty straightforward, just combine the two letters like you would in English.

OU / AU

These two vowel combinations sound exactly the same, and it sounds like the English 'ou' in 'house' or the 'o' in 'now'. The only difference is that in Dutch, you always make a Dutch 'w' sound after the 'ou' or 'au', which is quite similar to the combination of 'ow' in the English word 'now'.

Jou (you) YAU
// these words are quite similar. The 'j' sounds like the English 'y' in 'you'. The 'ou', however is not pronounced like the English 'oo' in 'choose', but like the 'ou' in 'house'.

Gebouw (building) guh-BAU
// the combination of the letters 'ouw' sound the same as the English 'ow' in 'now' or 'how'. Remember the guttural sounding 'g', and you've got this!

UI

There is no English equivalent to the Dutch vowel combination 'ui', but it sounds a bit like a combination of the sounds 'a', 'uu' and 'I' put together, but emphasize the 'uu' sound. In the phonetic descriptions we've left it as "UI" because there isn't an English equivalent, but please study and apply the pronunciation as explained below.

Tuin (garden) TUIN
// try to make a combination of the sounds 'a', 'uu' and 'I', and remember to emphasize the 'uu'.

Suiker (sugar) SUI-ker
// the 'ui' is pronounced the same as in the previous example. Remember to pronounce the 'e' as an 'uh' sound. With some practice, you will get this right!

EI / IJ

These vowel combinations are pronounced the same, and its pronunciation is somewhere in between 'fate' and 'fight'. The French have a similar sound, like the 'ei' in the city 'Marseille'. This might help you remember the sound of the Dutch 'ei' and 'ij'. Let's have a look at some examples.

Trein (train) TRAIN
// try to make an 'ei' sound that is in between 'fate' and 'fight'. The rest of the word is pronounced the same as in English.

Meisje (girl) MAIS-yuh
// the 'ei' is pronounced the same as in the previous example, somewhere in between 'fate' and 'fight'. The combination of the consonants 'sj' sounds like the 'sh' in the English word 'ship'.

Bonus notes on dialects

There are several distinctive dialects in Dutch. Most people in the Southern regions of the Netherlands speak Flemish, or Limburgish. This dialect has a much softer sound to it. This is because the Dutch language is closer related to the English language, and Flemish has more of a French influence. For example, they do not pronounce the 'g' as a guttural sound, but like a soft 'g'. It almost sounds like a hissing sound. They also use some different words than the Dutch vocabulary, although a Flemish person will most often understand you if you speak Dutch to them.

Besides Dutch and Flemish, there is another dialect that is an official language in the Netherlands: Frisian. It is spoken in the northern region of the Netherlands, the province of 'Friesland'. Roughly speaking, each province has its own dialect. But in fact, there are over 15 officially recognized dialects. However, do not let this confuse you, because these dialects all adhere to the same vocabulary and grammar rules. If you stick to the standard Dutch language, you will be able to communicate with everyone in the Netherlands. There is no need to familiarize yourself with any specific dialect, although you should not be surprised if someone uses a slightly different pronunciation than you have learned.

COLORS

Yellow
Geel
Geyl

Green
Groen

Groon

Blue
Blauw
Blauw

Red
Rood
Roht

Light blue
Licht blauw
Ligt blauw

Violet
Licht paars

Ligt pahrs

Pink
Roze
ROH-zuh

Brown
Bruin
Bruin

White
Wit
Vit

Black
Zwart
Zvahrt

Gray
Grijs
Grais

Gold
Goud
Gaut

Orange
Oranje
oh-RAHN-yuh

Silver
Zilver
SIL-fuhr

What color is that sign?
Welke kleur heeft dat bord?
VEL-kuh kluhr heyft daht bohrt?

Is the cartoon in color?
Is de cartoon in kleur?
Is duh car-TOON in kluhr?

Is this television show in color?
Is dit televisieprogramma in kleur?
Is dit tey-luh-VEE-zee pro-GRAH-mah in kluhr?

This is a red pen.
Dit is een rode pen.
Dit is uhn ROH-duh pen.

This piece of paper is blue.
Dit stuk papier is blauw.
Dit stuhk pah-PEER is blauw.

What color is that car?
Welke kleur heeft die auto?
VEL-kuh kluhr heyft dee AU-toh?

What color are your clothes?
Welke kleur is jouw kleding?
VEL-kuh kluhr is yau KLEY-ding?

Is this the right color?
Is dit de juiste kleur?

Is dit duh YUIS-tuh kluhr?

What color is the stop light?
Welke kleur heeft het stoplicht?
VEL-kuh kluhr heyft het STOP-ligt?

Does that color mean danger?
Betekent die kleur gevaar?
Buh-TEY-kent dee kluhr guh-FAHR?

That bird is red.
Die vogel is rood.
Dee VOH-guhl is roht.

What color is that animal?
Welke kleur heeft dat dier?
VEL-kuh kluhr heyft daht deer?

The sky is blue.
De lucht is blauw.
Duh lugt is blauw.

The clouds are white.
De wolken zijn wit.
Duh VOL-kuhn sain vit.

That paint is blue.
Die verf is blauw.
Dee ferf is blauw.

Press the red button.
Druk op de rode knop.
Druhk ohp duh ROH-duh knohp.

Don't press the red button.
Druk niet op de rode knop.
Druhk neet ohp duh ROH-duh knohp.

Black and White
Zwart en wit
Zvahrt en vit.

Look at all the colors.
Kijk naar alle kleuren.
Kaik nahr AH-luh KLUH-ruhn.

Is that a color television?
Is dat een kleurentelevisie?
Is daht uhn KLUH-ruhn tey-luh-VEE-zee?

What color do you see?
Welke kleur zie jij?
VEL-kuh kluhr zee yai?

Can I have the color blue?
Mag ik de kleur blauw?
Mahg ik duh kluhr blauw?

What colors do you have for these frames?
Welke kleuren heb je voor deze monturen?
VEL-kuh KLUH-ruhn heb yuh fohr DEY-zuh mohn-TOO-ruhn?

Don't go until the color is green.
Ga pas als de kleur groen is.
Gah pahs ahls duh kluhr groon is.

Colored pencils
Gekleurde potloden
Guh-KLUHR-duh POHT-loh-duhn

Coloring pens
Kleurpotloden
KLUHR-poht-loh-duhn

The sharpener is black.
De puntenslijper is zwart.
Duh PUHN-tuhn-slai-puhr is zvahrt.

Do you have this in another color?
Heb je dit in een andere kleur?
Heb yuh dit in uhn AHN-duh-ruh kluhr?

Do you have this in a darker color?
Heb je dit in een donkerder kleur?
Heb yuh dit in uhn DONG-kuhr-duhr kluhr?

Do you have this in a lighter color?
Heb je dit in een lichtere kleur?
Heb yuh dit in uhn LIG-tuh-ruh kluhr?

Can you paint my house blue?
Kun je mijn huis blauw schilderen?
Kuhn yuh main huis blauw SGIL-duh-ruhn?

Can you paint my car the same color?
Kun je mijn auto in dezelfde kleur schilderen?
Kuhn yuh main AU-toh in duh-ZELF-duh kluhr SGIL-duh-ruhn?

The flag has three different colors.
De vlag heeft drie verschillende kleuren.
Duh flahg heyft dree fer-SGIL-luhn-duh KLUH-ruhn.

Is the color on the flag red?
Is de kleur op de vlag rood?
Is duh kluhr op duh flag roht?

NUMBERS

Zero	**Nine**	**Eighteen**
Nul	Negen	Achttien
Nuhl	*NEY-guhn*	*AG-teen*
One	**Ten**	**Nineteen**
Een	Tien	Negentien
Eyn	*Teen*	*NEY-guhn-teen*
Two	**Eleven**	**Twenty**
Twee	Elf	Twintig
Tvey	*Elf*	*TVIN-tig*
Three	**Twelve**	**Twenty-one**
Drie	Twaalf	Eenentwintig
Dree	*Tvahlf*	*EYN-en-tvin-tig*
Four	**Thirteen**	**Twenty-two**
Vier	Dertien	Tweeëntwintig
Feer	*DER-teen*	*TWEY-en-tvin-tig*
Five	**Fourteen**	**Twenty-three**
Vijf	Veertien	Drieëntwintig
Faif	*FEER-teen*	*DREE-en-tvin-tig*
Six	**Fifteen**	**Twenty-four**
Zes	Vijftien	Vierentwintig
Zes	*FAIF-teen*	*FEER-en-tvin-tig*
Seven	**Sixteen**	**Twenty-five**
Zeven	Zestien	Vijfentwintig
ZEY-fuhn	*ZES-teen*	*FAIF-en-tvin-tig*
Eight	**Seventeen**	**Twenty-six**
Acht	Zeventien	Zesentwintig
Agt	*ZEY-vuhn-teen*	*ZES-en-tvin-tig*

Twenty-seven
Zevenentwintig
ZEY-vuhn-en-tvin-tig

Twenty-eight
Achtentwintig
AGT-en-tvin-tig

Twenty-nine
Negenentwintig
NEY-guhn-en-tvin-tig

Thirty
Dertig
DER-tig

Forty
Veertig
FEER-tig

Fifty
Vijftig
FAIF-tig

Sixty
Zestig
ZES-tig

Seventy
Zeventig
ZEY-vuhn-tig

Eighty
Tachtig
TAHG-tig

Ninety
Negentig
NEY-guhn-tig

One hundred
Honderd
HOHN-duhrt

Two hundred
Tweehonderd
Twey HOHN-duhrt

Five hundred
Vijfhonderd
FAIF HOHN-duhrt

One thousand
Duizend
DUI-zuhnt

One hundred thousand
Honderdduizend
HON-duhrt DUI-zuhnt

One million
Een miljoen
Eyn mil-YOON

One billion
Een miljard
Eyn mil-YART

What does that add up to?
Hoeveel is dat in totaal?
HOO-feyl is daht in toh-TAHL?

What number is on this paper?
Welk getal staat op dit papier?
Velk guh-TAHL staht ohp dit pah-PEER?

What number is on this sign?
Welk getal staat op dit bord?
Velk guh-TAL staht ohp dit bohrt?

Are these two numbers equal?
Zijn deze twee getallen gelijk?
Sain DEY-zuh tvey guh-TAHL-uhn guh-LAIK?

My social security number is one, two, three, four, five.
Mijn burgerservicenummer is een, twee, drie, vier, vijf.
Main BUHR-guhr-suhr-vis-nuhm-muhr is eyn, tvey, dree, veer, faif.

I'm going to bet five hundred euros.
Ik zet vijfhonderd euro in.
Ik zet FAIF-hohn-duhrt UH-roh in.

Can you count to one hundred for me?
Kun je voor mij tot honderd tellen?
Kuhn yuh fohr mai tot HOHN-duhrt TE-luhn?

I took fourteen steps.
Ik heb veertien stappen genomen.
Ik heb FEER-teen STAH-puhn guh-NOH-muhn.

I ran two kilometers.
Ik heb twee kilometer gerend.
Ik heb tvey KEY-loh-mey-tuhr guh-rend.

The speed limit is 30 km/h.
De snelheidslimiet is 30 km/u.
Duh SNEL-haits-lee-meet is DER-tuhg KEE-loh-mey-tuhr per uhr.

What are the measurements?
Wat zijn de afmetingen?
Vat sain duh AF-mey-ting-uhn?

Can you dial this number?
Kun je dit nummer bellen?
Kun yuh dit NUH-muhr BE-luhn?

One dozen.
Een dozijn.
Eyn doh-SAIN.

A half-dozen.
Een half dozijn.
Uhn half doh-SAIN.

How many digits are in the number?
Hoeveel cijfers staan er in dit getal?
HOO-feyl SAI-fuhrs stahn er in dit guh-TAHL?

My phone number is nine, eight, five, six, two, one, eight, seven, eight, eight.
Mijn telefoonnummer is negen, acht, vijf, zes, twee, een, acht, zeven, acht, acht.
Main tey-luh-FOHN-nuh-muhr is NEY-guhn, ahgt, faif, zes, tvey, eyn, ahgt, ZEY-fuhn, ahgt, ahgt.

The hotel's phone number is one, eight hundred, three, two, three, five, seven, five, five.
Het telefoonnummer van het hotel is één, achthonderd, drie, twee, drie, vijf, zeven, vijf, vijf.
Het tey-luh-FOHN-nuh-muhr fahn het hoh-TEL is eyn, AHGT-hon-duhrt, dree, tvey, dree, faif, ZEY-vuhn, faif, faif.

The taxi number is six, eight, one, four, four, four, five, eight, one, nine.
Het taxinummer is zes, acht, één, vier, vier, vier, vijf, acht, één, negen.
Het TAHK-see-nuhm-muhr is zes, ahgt, eyn, feer, feer, feer, faif, ahgt, eyn, NEY-guhn.

Call my hotel at two, one, four, seven, one, two, nine, five, seven, six.
Bel mijn hotel op twee, één, vier, zeven, één, twee, negen, vijf, zeven, zes.
Bel main hoh-TEL op tvey, eyn, feer, ZEY-vuhn, eyn, tvey, NEY-guhn, faif, ZEY-vuhn, zes.

Call the embassy at nine, eight, nine, eight, four, three, two, one, seven, one.
Bel de ambassade op negen, acht, negen, acht, vier, drie, twee, een, zeven, een.
Bel duh ahm-bah-SA-duh op NEY-guhn, ahgt, NEY-guhn, ahgt, feer, dree, tvey, eyn, ZEY-vuhn, eyn.

GREETINGS

Hi!
Hoi!
Hoy!

How's it going?
Hoe gaat het?
Hoo gaht het?

What's new?
Nog nieuws?
Nohg neews?

What's going on?
Wat gebeurt er?
Vaht guh-BUHRT er?

Home, sweet home.
Oost west, thuis best.
Ohst vest, tuis best.

Ladies and gentlemen, thank you for coming.
Dames en heren, bedankt voor uw komst.
DAH-muhs en HEY-ruhn, buh-DANKT fohr ew kohmst.

How is everything?
Hoe gaat alles?
Hoo gaht ah-LUHS?

Long time, no see.
Lang niet gezien.
Lahng neet guh-ZEEN.

It's been a long time.
Het is lang geleden.
Het is lahng guh-LEY-duhn.

It's been a while!
Het is een tijd geleden!
Het is uhn tait guh-LEY-duhn!

How is life?
Hoe staat het leven?
Hoo staht het LEY-vuhn?

How is your day?
Hoe gaat je dag?
Hoo gaht yuh dahg?

Good morning.
Goedemorgen.
Goo-duh-MOR-guhn.

It's been too long!
Het is te lang geleden!
Het is tuh lahng guh-LEY-duhn!

Good afternoon.
Goedemiddag.
Goo-duh-MI-dahg.

How long has it been?
Hoelang is het geweest?
Hoo-LAHNG is het guh-VEYST?

It's a pleasure to meet you.
Het is een genoegen om je te ontmoeten.
Het is uhn guh-NOO-guhn om yuh tuh ohnt-MOO-tuhn.

It's always a pleasure to see you.
Het is altijd een genoegen om je te zien.
Het is AHL-tait uhn guh-NOO-guhn om yuh tuh zeen.

Allow me to introduce Earl, my husband.
Sta me toe Earl, mijn man, voor te stellen.
Stah muh too Earl, main mahn, fohr tuh STE-luhn.

Goodnight.
Goedenacht.
GOO-duh-nahgt.

May I introduce my brother and sister?
Mag ik mijn broer en zus voorstellen?
Mahg ik main broor en zuhs FOHR-ste-luhn?

Good evening.
Goedenavond.
GOO-duhn-ah-fohnt.

What's happening?
Wat gebeurt er?
Vaht guh-BUHRT er?

Happy holidays!
Fijne feestdagen!
FAI-nuh FEYST-dah-guhn!

Are you alright?
Gaat het goed?
Gaht het goot?

Merry Christmas!
Vrolijk kerstfeest!
VROH-luhk KEHRST-feyst!

Where have you been hiding?
Waar heb jij je verstopt?
Vahr heb yai yuh ver-STOPT?

Happy New Year!
Gelukkig nieuwjaar!

Guh-LUK-kuhg neew-YAHR!

How is your night?
Hoe is je avond?

Hoo is yuh AH-fohnt?

What have you been up to all these years?
Wat heb je al die jaren gedaan?
Vaht heb yuh ahl dee YAH-ruhn guh-DAHN?

When was the last time we saw each other?
Wanneer hebben we elkaar voor het laatst gezien?
VAH-neyr HE-buhn vuh el-KAHR fohr het lahtst guh-ZEEN?

It's been ages since I've seen you.
Het is eeuwen geleden dat ik je heb gezien.
Het is EYW-uhn guh-LEY-duhn daht ik yuh heb guh-ZEEN.

How have things been going since I saw you last?
Hoe gaat het sinds ik je voor het laatst zag?
Hoo gaht het sints ik yuh fohr het lahtst zahg?

What have you been up to?
Wat heb je gedaan?
Vaht heb yuh guh-DAHN?

How are you doing?
Hoe gaat het met je?
Hoo gaht het met yuh?

Goodbye.
Doei
Dooeei

Are you okay?
Alles goed?
AH-luhs GOOT?

How's life been treating you?
Hoe behandelt het leven je?
Hoo buh-HAHN-duhlt het LEY-vuhn yuh?

I'm sorry.
Sorry.
SOH-ree

Excuse me.
Neem me niet kwalijk.
Neym muh neet KWAH-luhk.

See you later!
Tot ziens!
Tot zeens!

What's your name?
Wat is je naam?
Vaht is yuh nahm?

My name is Bill.
Mijn naam is Bill.
Main nahm is bil.

Pleased to meet you.
Aangenaam kennis te maken.
AHN-guh-nahm KE-nis tuh MAH-kuhn.

How do you do?
Hoe gaat het met u?
Hoo gaht het met oo?

How are things?
Hoe staat het ermee?
Hoo staht het er-MEY?

You're welcome.
Graag gedaan.
Grahg guh-DAHN.

It's good to see you.
Het is goed om je te zien.
Het is goot om yuh tuh zeen.

How have you been?
Hoe gaat het met je?
Hoo gaht het met yuh?

Nice to meet you.
Leuk je te ontmoeten.
Luhk yuh tuh ont-MOO-tuhn.

Fine, thanks. And you?
Goed, bedankt. En jij?
Goot, buh-DAHNKT. En yai?

Good day to you.
Goedendag.
GOO-duhn-dahg.

Come in, the door is open.
Kom binnen, de deur is open.
Kohm BI-nuhn, duh duhr is OH-puhn.

My wife's name is Sheila.
Mijn vrouw heet Sheila.
Main frauw heyt SHEE-lah.

I've been looking for you!
Ik was naar jou aan het zoeken!
Ik vahs nahr yau ahn het ZOO-kuhn!

Allow me to introduce myself. My name is Earl.
Sta me toe mezelf voor te stellen. Mijn naam is Earl.
Stah muh too muh-ZELF for tuh STE-luhn. Main nahm is Earl.

I hope you have enjoyed your weekend!
Ik hoop dat je van je weekend hebt genoten!
Ik hohp daht yuh fahn yuh WEE-kent hebt guh-NOH-tuhn!

It's great to hear from you.
Het is goed om van je te horen.
Het is goot om fahn yuh tuh HOH-ruhn.

I hope you are having a great day.
Ik hoop dat je een geweldige dag hebt.
Ik hohp daht yuh uhn guh-VEL-di-guh dahg hebt.

Thank you for your help.
Bedankt voor je hulp.
Buh-DAHNKT for yuh hulp.

DATE AND TIME

January
Januari
Yah-noo-AH-ree

February
Februari
Fey-broo-AH-ree

March
Maart
Mahrt

April
April
A-PRIL

May
Mei
Mai

June
Juni
YOO-nee

July
Juli
YOO-lee

August
Augustus
Au-GUHS-tuhs

September
September
Sep-TEM-buhr

October
Oktober
Ohk-TOH-buhr

November
November
Noh-VEM-buhr

December
December
Dey-SEM-buhr

What month is it?
Welke maand is het?
VEL-kuh mahnt is het?

At what time?
Op welk tijdstijp?
Ohp velk TAIT-stip?

Do you observe Daylight saving time?
Houdt u zich aan de zomertijd?
Haut oo zig aahn duh ZOH-muhr-tait?

The current month is January.
De huidige maand is januari.
Duh HUI-di-guh mahnt is yah-noo-AH-ree.

What day of the week is it?
Welke dag van de week is het?
VEL-kuh dahg fahn duh weyk is het?

Is today Tuesday?
Is het vandaag dinsdag?
Is het fahn-DAHG DINS-dahg?

Today is Monday.
Vandaag is het maandag.
Fahn-DAHG is het MAHN-dahg.

Is this the month of January?
Is het de maand januari?
Is het duh mahnt ya-noo-AH-ree?

It is five minutes past one.
Het is vijf minuten over een.
Het is faif mee-NOO-tuhn OH-fuhr eyn.

It is ten minutes past one.
Het is tien over een.
Het is teen OH-fuhr eyn.

It is ten till one.
Het is tien voor een.
Het is teen fohr eyn.

It is half past one.
Het is half twee.

Het is half tvey.

What time is it?
Hoe laat is het?
Hoo laht is het?

When does the sun go down?
Wanneer gaat de zon onder?
VAH-neyr gaht duh zon ON-duhr?

It's the third of November.
Het is drie November.
Het is dree noh-VEM-buhr.

When does it get dark?
Wanneer wordt het donker?
VAH-neyr wohrt het DONG-kuhr?

What is today's date?
Wat is de datum van vandaag?
Vaht is duh DAH-tuhm fahn fahn-DAHG?

What time does the shoe store open?
Hoe laat gaat de schoenenwinkel open?
Hoo laht gaht duh SGOO-nuhn-wing-kuhl OH-puhn?

Is today a holiday?
Is het vandaag een feestdag?
Is het fahn-DAHG uhn FEYST-dahg?

When is the next holiday?
Wanneer is de volgende feestdag?
VAH-neyr is duh FOHL-gun-duh FEYST-dahg?

I will meet you at noon.
Ik zie je om twaalf uur.
Ik zee yuh ohm tvahlf oor.

I will meet you later tonight.
Ik zie je later vanavond.
Ik zee yuh LAH-tuhr fahn-AH-fohnt.

My appointment is in ten minutes.
Mijn afspraak is over tien minuten.
Main AHF-sprahk is OH-fuhr teen mee-NOO-tuhn.

Can we meet in half an hour?
Kunnen we afspreken over een half uur?
KUH-nuhn vuh AHF-sprey-kuhn OH-fuhr uhn hahlf oor?

I will see you in March.
Ik zie je in maart.
Ik zee yuh in mahrt.

The meeting is scheduled for the twelfth.
De afspraak staat gepland voor de twaalfde.
Duh AF-sprahk staht guh-PLENT fohr duh TVAHLF-duh.

Can we set up the meeting for noon tomorrow?
Kunnen we de vergadering morgen om twaalf uur houden?
KUH-nuhn vuh duh vuhr-GAH-duh-ring MOHR-guhn om tvahlf oor HAU-duhn?

What time will the cab arrive?

Hoe laat komt de taxi?

Hoo laht komt duh TAHK-see?

Can you be here by midnight?

Kun je hier om twaalf uur 's nachts zijn?

Kuhn yuh heer ohm tvahlf oor snahgts sain?

The grand opening is scheduled for three o'clock.

De grote opening staat gepland voor drie uur.

Duh GROH-tuh OH-puh-ning staht guh-PLENT fohr dree oor.

When is your birthday?

Wanneer is je verjaardag?

VAH-neyr is yuh fuhr-YAHR-dahg?

My birthday is on the second of June.

Mijn verjaardag is op twee juni.

Main fuhr-YAHR-dahg is ohp tvey YOO-nee.

This place opens at ten a.m.

Deze plek opent om tien uur 's ochtends.

DEY-zuh plek OH-puhnt ohm teen oor SOHG-tuhnts.

From what time?

Vanaf hoe laat?

FAHN-AHF hoo laht?

Sorry, it is already too late at night.

Sorry, het is al te laat in de avond.

SOH-ree, het is ahl tuh laht in duh AH-fohnt.

COMMON QUESTIONS

Do you speak English?
Spreek je Engels?

Spreyk yuh ENG-uhls?

What is your hobby?
Wat is je hobby?
Vaht is yuh HOH-bee?

What language do you speak?
Welke taal spreek je?
VEL-kuh tahl spreyk yuh?

Was it hard?
Was het moeilijk?
Vahs het MOOI-luhk?

Can you help me?
Kun je mij helpen?
Kuhn yuh mai HEL-puhn?

Where can I find help?
Waar kan ik hulp vinden?
Vahr kahn ik huhlp FIN-duhn?

Where are we right now?
Waar zijn we nu?
Vahr sain vuh noo?

Where were you last night?
Waar was je gisteren?
Vahr vahs yuh GIS-tuh-ruhn?

What type of a tree is that?
Welke soort boom is dat?
VEL-kuh sohrt bohm is daht?

Do you plan on coming back here again?
Ben je van plan hier nog een keer terug te komen?
Ben yuh fahn plahn heer nohg uhn keyr tuh-RUHG tuh KOH-muhn?

What kind of an animal is that?
Wat voor dier is dat?
Vaht fohr deer is daht?

Is that animal dangerous?
Is dat dier gevaarlijk?
Is daht deer guh-VAHR-luhk?

Is it available?
Is het beschikbaar?
Is het buh-SGIK-bahr?

Can we come see it?
Kunnen we het komen bekijken?
KUH-nuhn vuh het KOH-muhn buh-KAI-kuhn?

Where do you live?
Waar woon je?
Wahr vohn yuh?

Earl, what city are you from?
Earl, uit welke stad kom jij?
Earl, uit VEL-kuh staht kohm yai?

Is it a very large city?
Is het een grote stad?
Is het uhn GROH-tuh staht?

Is there another available bathroom?
Is er nog een toilet vrij?
Is er nohg uhn toah-LET frai?

How was your trip?
Hoe was je reis?
Hoe was yuh rais?

Is the bathroom free?
Is het toilet vrij?
Is het twah-LET frai?

How are you feeling?
Hoe voel je je?
Hoo fool yuh yuh?

Do you have any recommendations?
Heb je aanbevelingen?
Heb yuh AHN-buh-vey-ling-uhn?

When did you first come to China?
Wanneer ben je voor het eerst naar China gekomen?
VAH-neyr ben yuh fohr het eyrst nahr SYEE-nah guh-KOH-muhn?

Were you born here?
Ben je hier geboren?
Ben yuh heer guh-boh-ruhn?

Come join me for the rest of the vacation.
Ga met me mee voor de rest van de vakantie.
Gah met muh mey fohr duh rest fahn duh vah-KAHN-see.

What times do the shops open in this area?
Hoe laat openen de winkels in dit gebied?
Hoo laht OH-pun-uhn duh WING-kuhls in dit guh-BEET?

Is there tax-free shopping available?
Kun je er belastingvrij winkelen?
Kuhn yuh er buh-LAHS-ting-frai WING-kuh-luhn?

Where can I change currency?
Waar kan ik buitenlands geld wisselen?
Wahr kahn ik BUI-tuhn-lahnds geld VI-suh-luhn?

Is it legal to drink in this area?
Is het legaal om te drinken in dit gebied?
Is het luh-GAHL ohm tuh DRING-kuhn in dit guh-BEET?

Can I smoke in this area?
Mag ik roken in dit gebied?
Mahg ik ROH-kuhn in dit guh-BEET?

What about this?
Hoe zit het hiermee?
Hoo zit het HEER-mey?

Can I park here?
Mag ik hier parkeren?
Mahg ik heer pahr-KEY-ruhn?

Have you gotten used to living in Spain by now?
Ben je al gewend om in Spanje te wonen?
Ben yuh ahl guh-VENT ohm in SPAHN-yuh tuh VOH-nuhn?

How much does it cost to park here?
Hoeveel kost het om hier te parkeren?
HOO-veyl kohst het ohm heer tuh pahr-KEY-ruhn?

How long can I park here?
Hoe lang kan ik hier parkeren?
Hoo lahng kahn ik heer pahr-KEY-ruhn?

Where can I get some directions?
Waar kan ik een routebeschrijving krijgen?
Vahr kahn ik uhn ROO-tuh-buh-sgrai-ving KRAI-guhn?

Can you point me in the direction of the bridge?
Kun je mij in de richting van de brug wijzen?
Kun yuh mai in duh RIG-ting fahn duh bruhg VAI-zuhn?

What can I do here for fun?
Wat is hier voor leuks te doen?
Vaht is heer for luhks tuh doon?

Is this a family-friendly place?
Is dit een familievriendelijke plek?
Is dit uhn fah-MEE-lee-VREEN-duh-luh-kuh plek?

Are kids allowed here?
Zijn kinderen hier toegestaan?
Sain KIN-duh-ruhn heer TOO-guh-stahn?

Where can I find the park?
Waar kan ik het park vinden?
Vahr kahn ik het pahrk VIN-duhn?

How do I get back to my hotel?
Hoe kom ik terug naar mijn hotel?
Hoo kohm ik tuh-RUHG nahr main hoh-TEL?

Where can I get some medicine?
Waar kan ik medicijnen krijgen?
Vahr kahn ik mey-dee-SAI-nuhn KRAI-guhn?

Is my passport safe here?
Is mijn paspoort veilig hier?
Is main PAHS-pohrt FAI-luhg heer?

Do you have a safe for my passport and belongings?
Heb je een kluis voor mijn paspoort en spullen?
Heb yuh uhn kluis fohr main PAHS-pohrt en SPUH-luhn?

Is it safe to be here past midnight?
Is het veilig om hier na middernacht te zijn?
Is het FAI-luhg ohm heer nah mi-duhr-NAGT tuh sain?

When is the best time to visit this shop?
Wat is het beste moment om deze winkel te bezoeken?
Vaht is het BES-tuh MOH-ment ohm DEY-zuh VING-kuhl tuh buh-ZOO-kuhn?

What is the best hotel in the area?
Wat is het beste hotel in dit gebied?
Vaht is het BES-tuh hoh-TEL in dit guh-BEET?

What attractions are close to my hotel?
Welke bezienswaardigheden zijn dichtbij mijn hotel?
VEL-kuh buh-zeens-WAHR-duhg-hey-duhn sain digt-BAI main hoh-TEL?

Do you have any advice for tourists?
Heb je advies voor toeristen?
Heb yuh at-FEES for too-RIS-tuhn?

Do you have a list of the top things to do in the area?
Heb je een lijst van dingen om te doen in de omgeving?
Heb yuh uhn laist fahn DING-uhn om tuh doon in duh ohm-GEY-ving?

What do I need to pack to go there?
Wat moet ik inpakken om daarheen te gaan?
Vaht moot ik IN-pah-kuhn ohm dahr-HEYN tuh gahn?

Can you recommend me some good food to eat?
Kun je me wat lekker eten aanraden?
Kun yuh muh vaht LE-kuhr EY-tuhn AHN-rah-duhn?

What should I do with my time here?
Wat zal ik doen met mijn tijd hier?
Vaht zahl ik doon met main tait heer?

What is the cheapest way to get from my hotel to the shop?
Wat is de goedkoopste manier om van mijn hotel naar de winkel te komen?
Vaht is duh good-KOHP-stuh mah-NEER ohm fahn main hoh-TEL nahr duh VING-kuhl tuh KOH-muhn?

What do you think of my itinerary?
Wat vind je van mijn reisschema?
Vaht vint yuh fahn main RAIS-gey-mah?

Does my phone work in this country?
Werkt mijn telefoon in dit land?
Verkt main tey-luh-FOHN in dit lahnt?

What is the best route to get to my hotel?
Wat is de beste route om naar mijn hotel te komen?
Vaht is duh BES-tuh ROO-tuh ohm nahr main hoh-TEL tuh KOH-muhn?

Will the weather be okay for outside activities?
Zal het weer goed zijn voor buitenactiviteiten?
Zahl het vehr goot sain fohr BUI-tuhn-ak-tee-vee-tai-tuhn?

Was that rude?
Was dat onbeleefd?
Vahs daht on-buh-LEYFT?

Where should I stay away from?
Waar moet ik weg van blijven?
Vahr moot ik veg fahn BLAI-vuhn?

What is the best dive site in the area?
Wat is de beste duiklocatie in dit gebied?
Vaht is duh BES-tuh DUIK-loh-kah-tsee in dit guh-BEET?

What is the best beach in the area?
Wat is het beste strand in dit gebied?
Vaht is het BES-tuh strahnt in dit guh-BEET?

Do I need reservations?
Heb ik een reservering nodig?
Heb ik uhn rey-suhr-FEY-ring NOH-duhg?

I need directions to the best local food.
Ik heb een routebeschrijving nodig naar het beste lokale restaurant.
Ik heb uhn ROO-tuh-buh-sgrai-ving NOH-duhg nahr het BES-tuh loh-KAH-luh res-toh-RAHNT.

What's your name?
Wat is je naam?
Vaht is yuh nahm?

Where is the nearest place to eat?
Wat is de dichtstbijzijnde plek om te eten?
Vaht is duh DIGTST-bai-sain-duh plek ohm tuh EY-tuhn?

Where is the nearest hotel?
Waar is het dichtstbijzijnde hotel?
Vahr is het DIGTST-bai-sain-duh hoh-TEL?

Where is transportation?
Waar is er vervoer?
Vahr is er vuhr-VOOR?

How much is this?
Hoeveel is dit?
HOO-veyl is dit?

Do you pay tax here?
Betaal je hier belasting?
Buh-TAHL yuh heer buh-LAHS-ting?

What types of payment are accepted?
Welke soorten betaling worden geaccepteerd?
VEL-kuh SOHR-tuhn buh-TAH-ling VOHR-duhn guh-AHK-suhp-tehrt?

Can you help me read this?
Kun je mij helpen om dit te lezen?
Kuhn yuh mai HEL-puhn ohm dit tuh LEY-zuhn?

What languages do you speak?
Welke talen spreek je?
VEL-kuh TAH-luhn spreyk yuh?

Is it difficult to speak English?
Is het moeilijk om Engels te spreken?
Is het MOOI-luhk ohm ENG-uhls tuh SPREY-kuhn?

What does that mean?
Wat betekent dat?
Vaht buh-TEY-kuhnt daht?

What is your name?
Wat is je naam?
Vaht is yuh nahm?

Do you have a lighter?
Heb je een aansteker?
Heb yuh uhn AHN-stey-kuhr?

Do you have a match?
Heb je een lucifer?
Heb yuh uhn LOO-see-fer?

Is this a souvenir from your country?
Is dit een souvenir uit jouw land?
Is dit uhn soo-vuh-NEER uit yau lahnt?

What is this?
Wat is dit?
Vaht is dit?

Can I ask you a question?
Mag ik je een vraag stellen?
Mag ik yuh uhn frahg STE-luhn?

Where is the safest place to store my travel information?
Wat is de veiligste plek om mijn reisinformatie te bewaren?
Vaht is duh FAI-luhg-stuh plek ohm main RAIS-in-for-mah-tsee tuh buh-WAH-ruhn?

Will you come along with me?
Kom je met me mee?
Kohm yuh met muh mey?

Is this your first time here?
Is dit je eerste keer hier?
Is dit yuh EYR-stuh keyr heer?

What is your opinion on the matter?
Wat is jouw mening hierover?
Vaht is yau MEY-ning heer-OH-fuhr?

Will this spoil if I leave it out too long?
Zal dit bederven als ik het te lang buiten de koelkast laat staan?
Zahl dit buh-DER-vuhn ahls ik het tuh lahng bui-tuhn duh KOOL-kahst laht stahn?

What side of the sidewalk do I walk on?
Aan welke kant van de stoep moet ik lopen?
Ahn VEL-kuh kahnt fahn duh stoop moot ik LOH-puhn?

What do those lights mean?
Wat betekenen die lichten?
Vaht buh-TEY-kuh-nuhn dee LIG-tuhn?

Can I walk up these stairs?
Mag ik deze trap oplopen?
Mahg ik DEY-zuh trahp OHP-loh-puhn?

Is that illegal here?
Is dat illegaal hier?
Is daht ee-luh-GAHL heer?

How much trouble would I get in if I did that?
Hoeveel problemen zou ik krijgen als ik dat zou doen?
HOO-veyl proh-BLEY-muhn zau ik KRAI-guhn ahls ik daht zau doon?

Why don't we all go together?
Waarom gaan we niet allemaal samen?
VAH-rohm gahn vuh neet ah-luh-MAHL SAH-muhn?

May I throw away waste here?
Mag ik hier afval weggooien?
Mahg ik heer AHF-vahl VEG-goh-yuhn?

Where is the recycle bin?
Waar is de prullenbak?
Vahr is duh PRUH-luhn-bahk?

WHEN SOMEONE IS BEING RUDE

Please, close your mouth while chewing that.
Sluit alsjeblieft je mond terwijl je daarop kauwt.
Sluit ahs-yuh-BLEEFT yuh mohnt tuhr-WAIL yuh DAHR-ohp kauwt.

Don't ask me again, please.
Vraag me het niet nog eens, alsjeblieft.

Vrahg muh het neet nohg eyns, ahs-yuh-BLEEFT.

I'm not paying for that.
Ik betaal daar niet voor.
Ik buh-TAHL dahr neet fohr.

Leave me alone or I am calling the authorities.
Laat me met rust, anders bel ik de politie.
Laht muh met ruhst, AHN-duhrs bel ik duh poh-LEET-see.

Hurry up!
Schiet op!
Sgeet ohp!

Stop bothering me!
Val me niet lastig!
Vahl muh neet LAHS-tuhg!

Don't bother me, please!
Val me niet lastig, alsjeblieft!
Vahl muh neet LAHS-tuhg, ahs-yuh-BLEEFT!

Are you content?
Ben je tevreden?
Ben yuh tuh-VREY-duhn?

I'm walking away, please don't follow me.
Ik loop weg, volg me alsjeblieft niet.
Ik lohp veg, fohlg muh ahs-yuh-BLEEFT neet.

You stole my shoes and I would like them back.
Je hebt mijn schoenen gestolen en ik wil ze graag terug.
Yuh hebt main SGOO-nuhn guh-STOH-luhn en ik vil zuh grahg tuh-RUHG.

You have the wrong person.
Je hebt de verkeerde persoon.
Yuh hebt duh fuhr-KEYR-duh per-SOHN.

I think you are incorrect.
Ik denk dat je ongelijk hebt.
Ik denk daht yuh ohn-guh-LAIK hebt.

Stop waking me up!
Stop met me wakker te maken!
Stohp met muh WAH-kuhr tuh MAH-kuhn!

You're talking too much.
Je praat teveel.
Yuh praht tuh-VEYL.

That hurts!
Dat doet pijn!
Daht doot pain!

I need you to apologize.
Je moet je verontschuldigen.
Yuh moot yuh fuhr-ofnt-SGUHL-duh-guhn.

Stay away from my children!
Blijf weg van mijn kinderen!
Blaif weg fahn main KIN-duh-ruhn!

Don't touch me.
Raak me niet aan.
Rahk muh neet ahn.

I would appreciate it if you didn't take my seat.
Ik zou het op prijs stellen als je mijn zitplaats niet inneemt.
Ik zau het ohp prais STE-luhn ahls yuh main ZIT-plahts neet IN-neymt.

You didn't tell me that.
Je hebt me dat niet verteld.
Yuh hebt muh daht neet fer-TELT.

You are price gouging me.
Je probeert geld van me af te troggelen.
Yuh proh-BEYRT gelt fahn muh ahf tuh TROH-guh-luhn.

Please be quiet, I am trying to listen.
Wees alsjeblieft stil, ik probeer te luisteren.
Veys ahs-yuh-BLEEFT stil, ik proh-BEYR tuh LUIS-tuh-ruhn.

Don't interrupt me while I am talking.
Onderbreek me niet als ik praat.
Ohn-duhr-BREYK muh neet ahls ik praht.

Don't sit on my car and stay away from it.
Zit niet op mijn auto, en blijf weg.
Zit neet ohp main AU-toh en blaif veg.

Get out of my car.
Kom uit mijn auto.
Kohm uit main AU-toh.

Get away from me and leave me alone!
Ga weg en laat me met rust!
Gah veg en laht muh met ruhst!

You're being rude.
Je bent onbeleefd.
Yuh bent ohn-buh-LEYFT.

Please don't curse around my children.
Scheld alsjeblieft niet in het bijzijn van mijn kinderen.
Sgelt ahs-yuh-BLEEFT neet in het BAi-sain fahn main KIN-duh-ruhn.

Let go of me!
Laat me los!
Laht muh lohs!

I'm not going to tell you again.
Ik ga het je niet nog een keer zeggen.
Ik gah het yuh neet nohg uhn keyr ZE-guhn.

Don't yell at me.
Schreeuw niet naar me.
Sgreyw neet nahr muh.

Please lower your voice.
Praat alsjeblieft wat zachter.
Praaht AHS-yuh-BLEEFT waht ZAHG-tuhr.

What is the problem?
Wat is het probleem?
Vaht is het proh-BLEYM?

I would appreciate if you didn't take pictures of me.
Ik zou het op prijs stellen als je geen foto's van me maakt.
Ik zau het ohp prais STE-luhn ahls yuh geyn FOH-tohs fahn muh mahkt.

I am very disappointed in the way you are behaving.
Ik ben erg teleurgesteld in de manier waarop je je gedraagt.
Ik ben erg tuh-LUHR-guh-stelt in duh mah-NEER vahr-OHP yuh yuh guh-DRAHGT.

Watch where you are walking!
Kijk waar je loopt!
Kaik vahr yuh lohpt!

He just bumped into me!
Hij botste tegen me aan!
Hai BOHT-stuh TEY-guhn muh ahn!

MEDICAL

I would like to set up an appointment with my doctor.
Ik wil graag een afspraak maken met mijn dokter.
Ik vil grahg uhn AHF-sprahk MAH-kuhn met main DOHK-tuhr.

I am a new patient and need to fill out forms.
Ik ben een nieuwe patiënt en moet formulieren invullen.
Ik ben uhn NEE-wuh pah-SYENT en moot fohr-moo-LEE-ruhn IN-vuh-luhn.

I am allergic to certain medications.
Ik ben allergisch voor bepaalde medicijnen.
Ik ben ah-LER-gees fohr buh-PAHL-duh mey-dee-SAI-nuhn.

That is where it hurts.
Dat is waar het pijn doet.
Daht is vahr het pain doot.

I have had the flu for three weeks.
Ik heb de afgelopen drie weken griep gehad.
Ik heb duh AHF-guh-loh-puhn dree VEY-kuhn greep guh-HAHT.

It hurts when I walk on that foot.
Het doet pijn als ik op die voet loop.
Het doot pain ahls ik ohp dee voot lohp.

When is my next appointment?
Wanneer is mijn volgende afspraak?
VAH-neyr is main FOHL-guhn-duh AHF-sprahk?

Does my insurance cover this?
Dekt mijn verzekering dit?
Dekt main fuhr-ZEY-kuh-ring dit?

Do you want to take a look at my throat?
Wilt u naar mijn keel kijken?
Vilt oo nahr main keyl KAI-kuhn?

Do I need to fast before going there?
Moet ik vasten voordat ik daarheen ga?
Moot ik VAHS-tuhn FOHR-daht ik dahr-HEYN gah?

Is there a generic version of this medicine?
Is er een generieke versie van dit medicijn?
Is er uhn gey-nuh-REE-kuh FER-see fahn dit mey-dee-SAIN?

I need to get back on dialysis.
Ik moet weer dialyse ondergaan.
Ik moot weyr dee-a-LEE-suh ohn-duhr-GAHN.

My blood type is A.
Mijn bloedgroep is A.
Main BLOOT-groop is AH.

I will be more than happy to donate blood.
Ik doneer graag bloed.
Ik doh-NEYR grahg bloot.

I have been feeling dizzy.
Ik voel me duizelig.
Ik fool muh DUI-zuh-luhg.

The condition is getting worse.
De toestand wordt erger.
Duh TOO-stahnt wohrt ER-guhr.

The medicine has made the condition a little better, but it is still there.
Het medicijn heeft de toestand een beetje beter gemaakt, maar het is er
nog steeds.
*Het mey-dee-SAIN heyft duh TOO-stahnt uhn BEY-tyuh BEY-tuhr guh-
MAHKT, mahr het is er nohg steyts.*

Is my initial health examination tomorrow?
Is mijn eerste gezondheidsonderzoek morgen?
Is main EYR-stuh guh-ZOHNT-haits-ohn-dur-zook MOHR-guhn?

I would like to switch doctors.
Ik wil graag van dokter wisselen.
Ik vil grahg fahn DOHK-tuhr VI-suh-luhn.

Can you check my blood pressure?
Kun je mijn bloeddruk controleren?
Kuhn yuh main BLOOT-druhk kohn-troh-LEY-ruhn?

I have a fever that won't go away.
Ik heb koorts en het gaat niet weg.
Ik heb kohrts en het gaht neet veg.

I think my arm is broken.
Ik denk dat mijn arm gebroken is.
Ik denk daht main ahrm guh-BROH-kuhn is.

I think I have a concussion.
Ik denk dat ik een hersenschudding heb.
Ik denk daht ik uhn HER-suhn-sguh-ding heb.

My eyes refuse to focus.
Mijn ogen willen niet focussen.
Main OH-guhn VI-luhn neet FOH-kuh-suhn.

I have double vision.
Ik zie dubbel.
Ik zee DUH-buhl.

Is surgery the only way to fix this?
Is een operatie de enige manier om dit op te lossen?
Is uhn oh-puh-RAH-tsee duh EY-nuh-guh mah-NEER ohm dit ohp tuh LOH-suhn?

Who are you referring me to?
Naar wie verwijs je me door?
Nahr vee vuhr-VAIS yuh muh dohr?

Where is the waiting room?
Waar is de wachtkamer?
Vahr is duh WAHGT-kah-muhr?

Can I bring someone with me into the office?
Kan ik iemand meenemen naar het kantoor?
Kahn ik EE-mahnt MEY-ney-muhn nahr het kahn-TOHR?

I need help filling out these forms.
Ik heb hulp nodig bij het invullen van deze formulieren.
Ik heb huhlp NOH-duhg bai het IN-vuh-luhn fahn DEY-zuh for-mew-LEE-ruhn.

Do you take Cobra as an insurance provider?
Accepteren jullie Cobra als verzekeringsmaatschappij?
Ahk-sep-TEY-ruhn YUH-lee KOH-brah ahls vuhr-ZEY-kuh-rings-maht-sgah-pai?

What is my copayment?
Hoeveel is mijn eigen bijdrage?
Hoo-FEYL is main AI-guhn BAI-dra-guh?

What forms of payment do you accept?
Welke vormen van betaling accepteren jullie?
VEL-kuh FOHR-muhn fahn buh-TAH-ling ahk-sep-TEY-ruhn YUH-lee?

Do you have a payment plan, or is it all due now?
Heeft u een betalingsregeling of moet u het allemaal meteen betaald worden?
Heyft oo uhn buh-TAH-lings-REY-guh-ling ohf moot ik het ah-luh-MAHL noo buh-TAAH-luhn?

My old doctor prescribed something different.
Mijn vorige dokter schreef me iets anders voor.
Main FOH-ruh-guh DOHK-tuhr sgreyf muh eets AHN-duhrs for.

Will you take a look at my leg?
Wil je naar mijn been kijken?
Vil yuh nahr main beyn KAI-kuhn?

I need to be referred to a gynecologist.
Ik moet worden doorverwezen naar een gynaecoloog.
Ik moot VOHR-duhn DOHR-vuhr-wey-zuhn nahr uhn gee-ne-koh-LOHG.

I am unhappy with the medicine you prescribed me.
Ik ben niet blij met het medicijn dat je me hebt voorgeschreven.
Ik ben neet blai met het mey-dee-SAIN daht yuh muh hebt FOR-guh-sgrey-vuhn.

Do you see patients on the weekend?
Ontvang je patiënten in het weekend?
Ohnt-FAHNG yuh pah-SYEN-tuhn in het VEE-kent?

I need a good therapist.
Ik heb een goede therapeut nodig.
Ik heb uhn GOO-duh tey-rah-PAUT NOH-duhg.

How long will it take me to rehab this injury?
Hoelang duurt het voordat ik van deze blessure ben hersteld?
HOO-lahng duhrt het FOR-daht ik fahn DEY-zuh ble-SOO-ruh ben her-STELT?

I have not gone to the bathroom in over a week.
Ik ben al meer dan een week niet naar de wc geweest.
Ik ben ahl meyr dahn uhn veyk neet nahr duh vey-SEY guh-VEYST.

I am constipated and feel bloated.
Ik ben verstopt en voel me opgeblazen.
Ik ben fuhr-STOHPT en fool muh OHP-guh-blah-zuhn.

It hurts when I go to the bathroom.
Het doet pijn als ik naar de wc ga.
Het doot pain ahls ik nahr duh vey-SEY gah.

I have not slept well at all since getting here.
Ik heb niet goed geslapen sinds ik hier ben aangekomen.
Ik heb neet good guh-SLAH-puhn sints ik heer ben AHN-guh-koh-muhn.

Do you have any pain killers?
Heb je pijnstillers?
Heb yuh PAIN-sti-luhrs?

I am allergic to that medicine.
Ik ben allergisch voor dat medicijn.
Ik ben ah-LER-gees fohr daht mey-dee-SAIN.

How long will I be under observation?
Hoelang zal ik geobserveerd worden?
HOO-lahng zahl ik guh-ohb-suhr-FEYRT VOHR-duhn?

I have a toothache.
Ik heb kiespijn.
Ik heb KEES-pain.

Do I need to see a dentist?
Moet ik een tandarts zien?
Moot ik uhn TAHN-dahrts zeen?

Does my insurance cover dental?
Dekt mijn verzekering tandzorg?
Dekt main fuhr-ZEY-kuh-ring TAHNT -zohrg?

My diarrhea won't go away.
Mijn diarree gaat niet weg.
Main dee-ya-REY gaht neet weg.

Can I have a copy of the receipt for my insurance?
Kan ik een kopie van het betalingsbewijs krijgen voor mijn verzekering?
Kahn ik uhn koh-PEE fahn het buh-TAH-lings-buh-vais KRAI-gun for main fuhr-ZEY-kuh-ring?

I need a pregnancy test.
Ik heb een zwangerschapstest nodig.
Ik heb uhn ZVAHNG-uhr-sgahps-test NOH-duhg.

I think I may be pregnant.
Ik denk dat ik zwanger ben.
Ik denk daht ik ZVAHNG-uhr ben.

Can we please see a pediatrician?
Kunnen we alsjeblieft een kinderarts zien?
KUN-uhn vuh ahs-yuh-BLEEFT uhn KIN-duhr-ahrts zeen?

I have had troubles breathing.
Ik heb moeite met ademen.
Ik heb MOOI-tuh met AH-duh-muhn.

My sinuses are acting up.
Mijn neusholtes zijn geïrriteerd.
Main NUHS-hohl-tuhs sain guh-ee-ree-TEYRD.

Will I still be able to breastfeed?
Zal ik nog steeds borstvoeding kunnen geven?
Zahl ik nohg steyts BOHRST-foo-ding KUH-nuhn GEY-vuhn?

How long do I have to stay in bed?
Hoelang moet ik in bed blijven?
HOO-lahng moot ik in bet BLAI-vuhn?

How long do I have to stay under hospital care?
Hoelang moet ik in het ziekenhuis blijven?
HOO-lahng moot ik in het ZEE-kuhn-huis BLAI-vuhn?

Is it contagious?
Is het besmettelijk?
Is het buh-SME-tuh-luhk?

How far along am I?
Hoe ver ben ik?
Hoo fer ben ik?

What did the x-ray say?
Wat was er op de röntgenfoto te zien?
Vaht vahs er ohp duh RUHNT-guhn-foh-toh tuh zeen?

Can I walk without a cane?
Kan ik lopen zonder stok?
Kahn ik LOH-puhn ZOHN-duhr stohk?

Is the wheelchair necessary?
Is de rolstoel nodig?
Is duh ROHL-stool NOH-duhg?

Am I in the right area of the hospital?
Ben ik in het juiste deel van het ziekenhuis?
Ben ik in het YUIS-tuh deyl fahn het ZEE-kuhn-huis?

Where is the front desk receptionist?
Waar is de receptioniste?
Vahr is duh ruh-sep-syoh-NIS-tuh?

I would like to go to a different waiting area.
Ik wil graag naar een andere wachtruimte gaan.
Ik wil grahg nahr uhn AHN-duh-ruh VAHGT-ruim-tuh gahn.

Can I have a change of sheets, please?
Mag ik schone lakens, alsjeblieft?
Mahg ik SGOH-nuh LAH-kuhns ahs-yuh-BLEEFT?

Excuse me, what is your name?
Pardon, hoe heet je?
Pahr-DOHN, hoo heyt yuh?

Who is the doctor in charge here?
Welke dokter heeft hier de leiding?
VEL-kuh DOHK-tuhr heyft heer duh LAI-ding?

I need some assistance, please.
Ik heb hulp nodig, alsjeblieft.
Ik heb huhlp NOH-duhg ahs-yuh-BLEEFT.

Will my recovery affect my ability to do work?
Heeft mijn herstel invloed op mijn vermogen om te werken?
Heyft main her-STEL IN-floot ohp main fuhr-MOH-guhn ohm tuh VER-kuhn?

How long is the estimated recovery time?
Hoelang is de geschatte hersteltijd?
HOO-lahng is duh guh-SGAH-tuh her-STEL-tait?

Is that all you can do for me? There has to be another option.
Is dat alles wat je voor me kunt doen? Er moet een andere optie zijn.
Is daht AH-luhs vaht yuh fohr muh kuhnt doon? Er moot uhn AHN-duh-ruh OHP-see sain.

I need help with motion sickness.
Ik heb hulp nodig bij reisziekte.
Ik heb huhlp NOH-duhg bai RAIS-zeek-tuh.

I'm afraid of needles.
Ik ben bang voor naalden.
Ik ben bahng fohr NAHL-duhn.

My gown is too small; I need another one.
Mijn ziekenhuishemd is te klein; ik heb een andere nodig.
Main ZEE-kuhn-huis-hemd is tuh klain, ik heb uhn AHN-duh-ruh NOH-duhg.

Can I have extra pillows?
Kan ik extra kussens krijgen?
Kahn ik EK-strah KUH-suhns KRAI-guhn?

I need assistance getting to the bathroom.
Ik heb hulp nodig om naar de wc te gaan.
Ik heb huhlp NOH-duhg ohm nahr duh vey-SEY tuh gahn.

Hi, is the doctor in?
Hoi, is de dokter er?
Hoy, is duh DOHK-tuhr er?

When should I schedule the next checkup?
Wanneer moet ik de volgende controle plannen?
VAH-neyr moot ik duh FOHL-guhn-duh kohn-TROH-luh PLE-nuhn?

When can I have these stitches removed?

Wanneer kunnen de hechtingen worden verwijderd?

VAH-neyr KUH-nuhn duh HEG-ting-uhn VOHR-duhn fuhr-VAI-duhrt?

Do you have any special instructions while I'm in this condition?

Heb je speciale instructies terwijl ik in deze toestand ben?

Heb yuh spey-SYA-luh in-STRUHK-sees ter-VAIL ik in DEY-zuh TOO-stahnt ben?

ORDERING FOOD

Can I see the menu?
Mag ik het menu zien?
Mahg ik het muh-NOO zeen?

I'm really hungry. We should eat something soon.
Ik heb veel honger. We moeten snel iets eten.
Ik heb veyl HONG-uhr. Vuh MOO-tuhn snel iets EY-tuhn.

Can I take a look in the kitchen?
Mag ik een kijkje nemen in de keuken?
Mahg ik uhn KAIK-yuh NEY-muhn in duh KUH-kuhn?

Can we see the drink menu?
Mogen we het drankmenu zien?
MOH-guhn vuh het DRAHNK-muh-noo zeen?

When can we be seated?
Wanneer kunnen we gaan zitten?
VAH-neyr KUH-nuhn vuh gahn ZI-tuhn?

This is very tender and delicious.
Dit is erg mals en heerlijk.
Dit is erg mahls en HEYR-luhk.

Do you serve alcohol?
Serveert u alcohol?
Ser-FEYRT oo AHL-koh-hohl?

I'm afraid our party can't make it.
Ik ben bang dat ons gezelschap het niet redt.
Ik ben bahng daht ohns guh-ZEL-sgahp het neet ret.

That room is reserved for us.
Die kamer is voor ons gereserveerd.
Dee KAH-muhr is fohr ohns guh-REY-suhr-feyrt.

Are there any seasonal favorites that you serve?
Heeft u seizoensgebonden favorieten?
Heyft oo sai-ZOONS-guh-bohn-duhn fah-voh-REE-tuhn?

Do you offer discounts for kids or seniors?
Biedt u kortingen aan voor kinderen of senioren?
Beet oo KOHR-ting-uhn ahn fohr KIN-duh-ruhn ohf sey-nee-YOH-ruhn?

I would like it filleted.
Ik zou het graag gefileerd willen hebben.
Ik zau het grahg guh-fee-LEYRT VI-luhn HE-buhn.

I would like to reserve a table for a party of four.
Ik wil graag een tafel voor vier reserveren.
Ik vil grahg uhn TAH-fuhl for feer rey-suhr-FEY-ruhn.

I would like to place the reservation under my name.
Ik wil de reservering onder mijn naam plaatsen.
Ik vil duh rey-suhr-FEY-ring ON-dur main nahm PLAHT-suhn.

What type of alcohol do you serve?
Welk type alcohol serveert u?
Velk TEE-puh AHL-koh-hohl ser-FEYRT oo?

Do I need a reservation?
Heb ik een reservering nodig?
Heb ik uhn rey-suhr-FEY-ring NOH-duhg?

What does it come with?
Wat zit er bij?
Vaht zit er bai?

What are the ingredients?
Wat zijn de ingrediënten?
Vaht sain duh in-grey-dee-YEN-tuhn?

What else does the chef put in the dish?
Wat doet de chef nog meer in het gerecht?
Vaht doot duh syef nohg meyr in het guh-REGT?

I wonder which of these tastes better?
Ik vraag me af welke beter smaakt?
Ik vrahg muh ahf VEL-kuh BEY-tuhr smahkt?

That is incorrect. Our reservation was at noon.
Dat is niet juist. Onze reservering was om 12 uur.
Daht is neet yuist. OHN-zuh rey-suhr-FEY-ring vahs ohm tvahlf oor.

I would like red wine, please.
Ik wil graag rode wijn alstublieft.
Ik vil grahg ROH-duh vain ahs-too-BLEEFT.

Can you choose the soup?
Kan je de soep kiezen?
Kahn yuh duh soop KEE-zuhn?

What is the most popular dish here?
Wat is het meest populaire gerecht hier?
Vaht is het meyst poh-poo-LAIR-uh guh-REGT heer?

What are the specials today?
Wat zijn de gerechten van de dag?
Vaht sain duh guh-REG-tuhn fahn duh dahg?

What are your appetizers?
Wat zijn uw voorgerechten?
Vaht sain ew FOR-guh-reg-tuhn?

Please bring these out separately.
Deze graag apart brengen, alsjeblieft.
DEY-zuh grahg ah-PAHRT BRENG-uhn ahs-yuh-BLEEFT.

Do we leave a tip?
Laten we fooi achter?
LAH-tuhn vuh foy AHG-tuhr?

Are tips included with the bill?
Is de fooi bij de rekening inbegrepen?
Is duh foy bai duh REY-kuh-ning IN-buh-grey-puhn?

Split the bill, please.
Deel de rekening door twee alstublieft.
Deyl duh REY-kuh-ning dohr tvey ahs-too-BLEEFT.

We are paying separately.
We betalen apart.
Vuh buh-TAH-luhn ah-PAHRT.

Is there an extra fee for sharing an entrée?

Zijn er extra kosten verbonden aan het delen van een hoofdgerecht?

Sain er EK-strah KOHS-tuhn fuhr-BOHN-duhn ahn het DEY-luhn fahn uhn HOHFT-guh-regt?

Is there a local specialty that you recommend?

Is er een lokale specialiteit die u aanbeveelt?

Is er uhn loh-KAH-luh spey-sya-lee-TAIT dee ew AHN-buh-feylt?

This looks different from what I originally ordered.

Dit ziet er anders uit dan wat ik heb besteld.

Dit zeet er AHN-duhrs uit dahn vaht ik heb buh-STELT.

Is this a self-serve buffet?

Is dit een zelfbedieningsbuffet?

Is dit uhn ZELF-buh-dee-nings-boo-fet?

I want a different waiter.

Ik wil een andere ober.

Ik vil uhn AHN-duh-ruh OH-buhr.

Please move us to a different table.

Verplaats ons alstublieft naar een andere tafel.

Fuhr-PLAHTS ohns ahs-too-BLEEFT nahr uhn AHN-duh-ruh TAH-fuhl.

Can we put two tables together?

Kunnen we twee tafels bij elkaar zetten?

KUH-nuhn vuh tvey TAH-fuhls bai el-KAHR ZE-tuhn?

My spoon is dirty. Can I have another one?

Mijn lepel is vies. Mag ik een andere?

Main LEY-puhl is fees. Mahg ik uhn AHN-duh-ruh?

We need more napkins, please.

We hebben meer servetten nodig.

Vuh HE-buhn meyr ser-FE-tuhn NOH-duhg.

I'm a vegetarian and don't eat meat.

Ik ben vegetariër en eet geen vlees.

Ik ben fey-guh-TAH-ree-yuhr en eyt geyn fleys.

The table next to us is being too loud. Can you say something?

De tafel naast ons maakt te veel lawaai. Kunt u iets tegen hen zeggen?

Duh TAH-fuhl nahst ohns mahkt tuh fehl lah-VAHEE. Kuhnt oo eets TEY-guhn hen ZE-guhn?

Someone is smoking in our non-smoking section.
Iemand rookt in onze rookvrije sectie.
EE-mahnt rohkt in OHN-zuh ROHK-frai-yuh SEK-see.

Please seat us in a booth.
Geef ons alstublieft een tafel met bankjes.
Geyf ohns ahs-too-BLEEFT uhn TAH-fuhl met BAHNK-yuhs.

Do you have any non-alcoholic beverages?
Heeft u alcoholvrije dranken?
Heyft oo AHL-koh-hohl-frai-yuh DRANG-kuhn?

Where is your bathroom?
Waar is de WC?
Vahr is duh vey-SEY?

Are you ready to order?
Bent u klaar om te bestellen?
Bent oo klahr ohm tuh buh-STE-luhn?

Five more minutes, please.
Nog vijf minuten alstublieft.
Nohg faif mee-NOO-tuhn ahs-too-BLEEFT.

What time do you close?
Hoelaat gaan jullie dicht?
HOO-laht gahn YUH-lee digt?

Is there pork in this dish? I don't eat pork.
Zit er varkensvlees in dit gerecht? Ik eet geen varkensvlees.
Zit er FAHR-kuhns-fleys in dit guh-REGT? Ik eyt geyn FAHR-kuhns-fleys.

Do you have any dishes for vegans?
Heeft u gerechten voor veganisten?
Heyft oo guh-REG-tuhn fohr fey-gah-NIS-tuhn?

Are these vegetables fresh?
Zijn deze groenten vers?
Sain DEY-zuh GROON-tuhn fers?

Have any of these vegetables been cooked in butter?
Is een van deze groenten in boter gebakken?
Is eyn fahn DEY-zuh GROON-tuhn in BOH-tuhr guh-BAH-kuhn?

Is this spicy?
Is dit pittig?
Is dit PI-tig?

Is this sweet?
Is dit zoet?
Is dit zoot?

I want more, please.
Ik wil meer alstublieft.
Ik vil meyr ahs-too-BLEEFT.

I would like a dish containing these items.
Ik wil een gerecht met deze ingrediënten.
Ik vil uhn guh-REGT met DEY-zuh in-grey-dee-YEN-tuhn.

Can you make this dish light? Thank you.
Kunt u dit gerecht light maken? Dank u.
Kuhnt oo dit guh-REGT liet mah-kuhn? Dahnk oo.

Nothing else.
Verder niets.
FER-duhr neets.

Please clear the plates.
Neem de borden mee, alstublieft.
Neym duh BOHR-duhn mey, ahs-too-BLEEFT.

May I have a cup of soup?
Mag ik een kopje soep?
Mahg ik uhn KOHP-yuh soop?

Do you have any bar snacks?
Heeft u snacks?
Heyft oo sneks?

Another round, please.
Nog een rondje, alstublieft.
Nohg uhn ROHNT-yuh ahs-too-BLEEFT.

When is closing time for the bar?
Hoe laat sluit de bar?
Hoo laht sluit duh bahr?

That was delicious!
Dat was heerlijk!
Daht vahs HEYR-luhk!

Does this have alcohol in it?
Zit hier alcohol in?
Zit heer AHL-koh-hohl in?

Does this have nuts in it?
Zitten er noten in?
ZI-tuhn er NOH-tuhn in?

Is this gluten free?
Is dit glutenvrij?
Is dit gloo-tuhn-FRAI?

Can I get this to go?
Kunt u dit inpakken om mee te nemen?
Kuhnt oo dit in-PAH-kuhn ohm mey tuh NEY-muhn?

May I have a refill?
Mag ik er nog een?
Mahg ik er nohg eyn?

Is this dish kosher?
Is dit gerecht koosjer?
Is dit guh-REGT KOH-syuhr?

I would like to change my drink.
Ik wil mijn drankje veranderen.
Ik vil main DRANK-yuh fuhr-AHN-duh-ruhn.

My coffee is cold. Could you please warm it up?
Mijn koffie is koud. Kunt u het alstublieft opwarmen?
Main KOH-fee is kaut. Kuhnt oo het ahs-too-BLEEFT OHP-vahr-muhn?

Do you serve coffee?
Serveert u koffie?
Ser-FEYRT oo KOH-fee?

Can I please have cream in my coffee?
Mag ik alstublieft room in mijn koffie?
Mahg ik ahs-too-BLEEFT rohm in main KOH-fee?

Please add extra sugar to my coffee.
Voeg alstublieft extra suiker toe aan mijn koffie.
Foog ahs-too-BLEEFT EK-strah SUI-kuhr too ahn main KOH-fee.

I would like to have my coffee served black, no cream and no sugar.
Ik wil graag dat mijn koffie zwart wordt geserveerd, zonder room en zonder suiker.
Ik vil grahg daht main KOH-fee zvahrt vohrt guh-ser-FEYRT, ZOHN-duhr rohm en ZOHN-duhr SUI-kuhr.

I would like to have decaffeinated coffee, please.
Ik wil graag cafeïnevrije koffie, alstublieft.
Ik vil grahg kah-fey-EE-nuh-frai-yuh KOH-fee, ahs-too-BLEEFT.

Do you serve coffee-flavored ice cream?
Serveert u ijs met koffiesmaak?
Ser-FEYRT oo ais met KOH-fee-smahk?

Please put my cream and sugar on the side so that I can add it myself.
Doe alstublieft mijn room en suiker ernaast zodat ik het er zelf in kan doen.
Doo ahs-too-BLEEFT main rohm en SUI-kuhr er-NAHST zoh-DAHT ik het er zelf in kahn doon.

I would like to order an iced coffee.
Ik wil graag een ijskoffie bestellen.
Ik vil grahg uhn AIS-koh-fee buh-STE-luhn.

I would like an espresso please.
Ik wil graag een espresso.
Ik vil grahg uhn es-PRE-soh.

Do you have 2% milk?
Heeft u melk met 2% vet?
Heyft oo melk met tvey proh-SENT fet?

Do you serve soy milk?
Serveert u sojamelk?
Ser-FEYRT oo SOH-yah-melk?

Do you have almond milk?
Heeft u amandelmelk?
Heyft oo ah-MAHN-duhl-melk?

Are there any alternatives to the milk you serve?
Zijn er alternatieven voor de melk die u serveert?
Sain er ahl-tuhr-nah-TEE-vuhn fohr duh melk die oo ser-FEYRT?

Please put the lemons for my tea on the side.
Leg de citroen voor mijn thee ernaast, alstublieft.
Leg duh see-TROON fohr main tey er-NAHST, ahs-too-BLEEFT.

No lemons with my tea, thank you.
Geen citroen bij mijn thee, dank u.
Geyn see-TROON bai main tey, dank oo.

Is your water from the tap?
Komt uw water uit de kraan?
Kohmt ew VAH-tuhr uit duh krahn?

Sparkling water, please.
Bruisend water, alstublieft.
BRUI-suhnt VAH-tuhr ahs-too-BLEEFT.

Can I get a diet coke?
Mag ik een cola light?
Mahg ik uhn KOH-lah liet?

We're ready to order.
We zijn klaar om te bestellen.
Vuh sain klahr ohm tuh buh-STE-luhn.

Can we be seated over there instead?
Kunnen we eventueel aan die tafel daar zitten?
KUH-nuhn vuh ey-fen-too-EYL ahn dee TAH-fuhl dahr ZI-tuhn?

Can we have a seat outside?
Kunnen we een tafel buiten krijgen?
KUH-nuhn vuh uhn TAH-fuhl BUI-tuhn KRAI-guhn?

Please hold the salt.
Geen zout alstublieft.
Geyn zaut ahs-too-BLEEFT.

This is what I would like for my main course.
Dit is wat ik wil bestellen voor mijn hoofdgerecht.
Dit is vaht ik vil buh-STE-luhn fohr main HOHFT-guh-regt.

I would like the soup instead of the salad.
Ik wil de soep in plaats van de salade.
Ik vil duh soop in plahts fahn duh sah-LAH-duh.

I'll have the chicken risotto.
Ik neem de kiprisotto.
Ik neym duh KIP-ree-soh-toh.

Can I change my order?
Kan ik mijn bestelling wijzigen?
Kahn ik main buh-STE-ling VAI-zuh-guhn?

Do you have a kids' menu?
Heeft u een kindermenu?
Heyft oo uhn KIN-duhr-muh-noo?

When does the lunch menu end?
Tot hoe laat serveert u het lunchmenu?
Toht hoo laht ser-FEYRT oo het LUHNSH-muh-noo?

When does the dinner menu start?
Hoe laat begint het dinermenu?
Hoo laht buh-gint het dee-NEY-muh-noo?

Do you have any recommendations from the menu?
Heeft u aanbevelingen uit het menu?
Heyft oo AHN-buh-fey-ling-uhn uit het muh-NOO?

I would like to place an off-menu order.
Ik wil graag iets bestellen dat niet op het menu staat.
Ik vil grahg eets buh-STE-luhn daht neet ohp het muh-NOO staht.

Can we see the dessert menu?
Mogen we het dessertmenu zien?
MOH-guhn vuh het duh-SER-muh-noo zeen?

Is this available sugar-free?
Is dit suikervrij beschikbaar?
Is dit sui-kuhr-FRAI buh-SGIK-bahr?

May we have the bill, please?
Mogen wij de rekening alstublieft?
MOH-guhn vai duh REY-kuh-ning ahs-too-BLEEFT.

Where do we pay?
Waar moeten we betalen?
Vahr MOO-tuhn vuh buh-TAH-luhn?

Hi, we are with the party of Isaac.
Hallo, we zijn met het gezelschap van Isaac.
HAH-loh, vuh sain met het guh-ZEL-sgap fahn EE-sahk.

We haven't made up our minds yet on what to order. Can we have a few more minutes, please?
We hebben nog geen keuze kunnen maken. Mogen we nog een paar minuten hebben?
Vuh HE-buhn nohg geyn KUH-zuh KUH-nuhn MAH-kuhn. MOH-guhn vuh nohg uhn pahr mee-NOO-tuhn HE-buhn?

Waiter!
Ober!
OH-buhr!

Waitress!
Serveerster!
Ser-FEYR-stuhr!

I'm still deciding, come back to me, please.
Ik heb nog niet besloten, kom alstublieft terug.
Ik heb nohg neet buh-SLOH-tuhn, kohm ahs-too-BLEEFT tuh-RUHG.

Can we have a pitcher of that?
Mogen we daar een kan van hebben?
MOH-guhn vuh dahr uhn kahn van HE-bun?

This is someone else's meal.
Dit is de bestelling van iemand anders.
Dit is duh buh-STE-ling fahn EE-mahnt AHN-duhrs.

Can you please heat this up a little more?
Kunt u dit alstublieft wat meer opwarmen?
Kuhnt oo dit ahs-too-BLEEFT vaht meyr OHP-vahr-muhn?

I'm afraid I didn't order this.
Ik ben bang dat ik dit niet heb besteld.
Ik ben bahng daht ik dit neet heb buh-STELT.

The same thing again, please.
Hetzelfde graag.
Het-ZELF-duh grahg.

Can we have another bottle of wine?
Mogen wij nog een fles wijn?
MOH-guhn vai nohg uhn fles vain?

That was perfect, thank you!
Dat was perfect, dank u!
Daht vahs per-FEKT, dahnk oo!

Everything was good.
Alles was goed.
AH-luhs vahs goot.

Can we have the bill?
Mogen we de rekening?
MOH-guhn vuh duh REY-kuh-ning?

I'm sorry, but this bill is incorrect.
Sorry, maar deze rekening is niet juist.
SOH-ree, mahr DEY-zuh rey-KUH-ning is neet yuist.

Can I have clean cutlery?
Mag ik schoon bestek?
Mahg ik sgohn buh-STEK?

Can we have more napkins?
Mogen we wat meer servetten?
MOH-guhn vuh vaht meyr ser-FE-tuhn?

May I have another straw?
Mag ik nog een rietje?
Mahg ik nohg uhn REET-yuh?

What sides can I have with that?
Welke bijgerechten kan ik daarbij krijgen?
VEL-kuh BAI-guh-reg-tuhn kahn ik dahr-BAI KRAI-guhn?

Excuse me, but this is overcooked.
Pardon, maar dit is te gaar.
Pahr-DOHN, mahr dit is tuh gahr.

May I talk to the chef?
Mag ik de chef spreken?
Mahg ik duh syef SPREY-kuhn?

We have booked a table for fifteen people.
We hebben een tafel gereserveerd voor vijftien personen.
Vuh HE-buhn uhn TAH-fuhl guh-REY-suhr-feyrt fohr FAIF-teen per-SOH-nuhn.

Are there any tables free?
Zijn er nog tafels vrij?
Sain er nog TAH-fuhls frai?

I would like one beer, please.
Ik wil graag een biertje, alstublieft.
Ik vil grahg uhn BEER-tyuh, ahs-too-BLEEFT.

Can you add ice to this?
Kunt u hier ijs bij doen?
Kuhnt oo heer ais bai doon?

I would like to order a dark beer.
Ik wil graag een donker biertje bestellen.
Ik vil grahg uhn DOHNG-kuhr BEER-tyuh buh-STE-luhn.

Do you have any beer from the tap?
Heb je bier van de tap?
Heb yuh beer fahn duh tahp?

How expensive is your champagne?
Hoe duur is uw champagne?
Hoo duhr is ew syahm-PAHN-yuh?

Enjoy your meal.
Geniet van je maaltijd.
Guh-NEET fahn yuh MAHL-tait.

I want this.
Ik wil dit.
Ik vil dit.

Please cook my meat well done.
Ik wil mijn vlees goed doorbakken, alstublieft.
Ik vil main fleys goot dohr-BAH-kuhn, ahs-too-BLEEFT.

Please cook my meat medium rare.
Bak mijn vlees medium rood, alstublieft.
Bahk main fleys MEY-dee-yuhm roht, ahs-too-BLEEFT.

Please prepare my meat rare.
Bereid mijn vlees rood, alstublieft.
Buh-RAIT main fleys roht, ahs-too-BLEEFT.

What type of fish do you serve?
Wat voor soort vis serveert u?
Vaht fohr sohrt fis suhr-FEYRT oo?

Can I make a substitution with my meal?
Kan ik iets in mijn maaltijd vervangen?
Kahn ik eets in main MAHL-tait fuhr-FAHNG-uhn?

Do you have a booster seat for my child?
Heeft u een stoelverhoger voor mijn kind?
Heyft oo uhn STOOL-vuhr-hoh-guhr fohr main kint?

Call us when you get a table.
Bel ons als je een tafel krijgt.
Bel ohns ahls yuh un TAH-fuhl kraigt.

Is this a non-smoking section?
Is dit een rookvrij gedeelte?
Is dit uhn ROHK-frai guh-DEHL-tuh?

We would like to be seated in the smoking section.
We willen graag plaatsnemen in het rookgedeelte.
Vuh VI-luhn grahg PLAHTS-ney-muhn in het ROHK-guh-deyl-tuh.

This meat tastes funny.
Dit vlees smaakt raar.
Dit fleys smahkt rahr.

More people will be joining us later.
Later komen er meer mensen bij.
LAH-tuhr KOH-muhn er meyr MEN-suhn bai.

TRANSPORTATION

Where's the train station?
Waar is het treinstation?
Vahr is het TRAIN-stah-syohn?

How much does it cost to get to this address?
Hoeveel kost het om naar dit adres te komen?
Hoo-FEYL kohst het ohm nahr dit ah-DRES tuh KOH-muhn?

What type of payment do you accept?
Welke betalingswijzen accepteert u?
VEL-kuh buh-TAH-lings-VAI-zuhn ahk-sep-TEYRT u?

Do you have first-class tickets available?
Heeft u eerste klas kaarten beschikbaar?
Heyft oo EYR-stuh klahs KAHR-tuhn buh-SGIK-bahr?

What platform do I need to be on to catch this train?
Op welk platform moet ik zijn om deze trein te halen?
Ohp velk PLAHT-fohrm moot ik sain ohm DEY-zuh train tuh HAH-luhn?

Are the roads paved in this area?
Zijn de wegen in dit gebied verhard?
Sain duh VEY-guhn in dit guh-BEET fuhr-HAHRT?

Where are the dirt roads, and how do I avoid them?
Waar zijn de onverharde wegen en hoe vermijd ik ze?
Vahr sain duh OHN-fuhr-hahr-duh WEY-guhn en hoo fuhr-MAIT ik zuh?

Are there any potholes I need to avoid?
Zijn er kuilen die ik moet vermijden?
Sain er KUI-luhn dee ik moot fuhr-MAI-duhn?

How fast are you going?
Hoe hard ga je?
Hoo hahrt gah yuh?

Do I need to put my emergency blinkers on?
Moet ik mijn alarmlichten aandoen?
Moot ik main ah-LAHRM-ligt-uhn AHN-doon?

Make sure to use the right turn signals.
Zorg ervoor dat u de juiste richtingaanwijzers gebruikt.
Zohrg er-FOHR daht oo duh YUIS-tuh RIG-ting-ahn-vai-zuhrs guh-BRUIKT.

We need a good mechanic.
We hebben een goede monteur nodig.
Vuh HE-buhn uhn GOO-duh mohn-TUHR NOH-dug.

Can we get a push?
Kunnen we een duwtje krijgen?
KUH-nuhn vuh uhn DOOW-tyuh KRAI-guhn?

I have to call the towing company to move my car.
Ik moet het sleepbedrijf bellen om mijn auto te verplaatsen.
Ik moot het SLEYP-buh-draif BE-luhn ohm main AU-toh tuh fuhr-PLAHT-suhn.

Make sure to check the battery and spark plugs for any problems.
Zorg ervoor dat u de batterij en bougies controleert op problemen.
Zohrg er-FOHR daht oo duh bah-tuh-RAI en boo-zyees kohn-troh-LEYRT ohp proh-BLEY-muhn.

Check the oil level.
Controleer het oliepeil.
Kohn-troh-LEYR het OH-lee-pail.

I need to notify my insurance company.
Ik moet mijn verzekeringsmaatschappij op de hoogte stellen.
Ik moot main fuhr-ZEY-kuh-rings-maht-sgah-pai ohp duh HOHG-tuh STE-luhn.

When do I pay the taxi driver?
Wanneer betaal ik de taxichauffeur?
Vah-NEYR buh-TAHL ik duh TAHK-see-syau-fuhr?

Please take me to the nearest train station.
Breng me alstublieft naar het dichtstbijzijnde treinstation.
Breng muh ahs-too-BLEEFT nahr het DIGTST-bai-zain-duh TRAIN-stah-syohn.

How long does it take to get to this address?
Hoe lang duurt het om op dit adres te komen?
Hoo lahng duhrt het ohm ohp dit ah-DRES tuh KOH-muhn?

Can you stop here, please?
Kunt u hier alstublieft stoppen?
Kuhnt oo heer ahs-too-BLEEFT STOH-puhn?

You can drop me off anywhere around here.
Je kunt me hier overal afzetten.
Yuh kuhnt muh heer OH-vuh-rahl AHF-ze-tuhn.

Is there a charge for extra passengers?
Zijn er kosten verbonden aan extra passagiers?
Sain er KOHS-tuhn fer-BOHN-duhn ahn EK-strah pah-sah-ZYEERS?

What is the condition of the road? Is it safe to travel there?
Wat is de toestand van de weg? Is het veilig om daarheen te reizen?
Vaht is de TOO-stahnt fahn duh weg? Is het FAI-luhg ohm dahr-HEYN tuh RAI-zuhn?

Take me to the emergency room.
Breng me naar de eerste hulp.
Breng muh nahr duh EYR-stuh hulp.

Take me to the embassy.
Breng me naar de ambassade.
Breng muh nahr duh ahm-bah-SAH-duh.

I want to travel around the country.
Ik wil door het land reizen.
Ik vil dohr het lahnt RAI-zuhn.

Is this the right side of the road?
Is dit de juiste kant van de weg?
Is dit duh YUI-stuh kahnt fahn duh veg?

My car broke down, please help!
Mijn auto is stuk, help alstublieft!
Main AU-toh is stuhk, help ahs-too-BLEEFT!

Can you help me change my tire?
Kunt u mij helpen mijn band te vervangen?
Kuhnt oo mai HEL-puhn main bahnt tuh fuhr-FAHNG-uhn?

Where can I get a rental car?
Waar kan ik een huurauto krijgen?
Vahr kahn ik uhn HEWR-au-toh KRAI-guhn?

Please take us to the hospital.
Breng ons alstublieft naar het ziekenhuis.
Breng ohns ahs-too-BLEEFT nahr het ZEE-kuhn-huis.

Is that the car rental office?
Is dat het autoverhuurkantoor?
Is daht het AU-toh-ver-hewr-kahn-tohr?

May I have a price list for your fleet?
Mag ik een prijslijst hebben voor uw vloot?
Mahg ik uhn PRAIS-laist HE-buhn fohr ew floht?

Can I get insurance on this rental car?
Kan ik een verzekering afsluiten voor deze huurauto?
Kahn ik uhn fuhr-ZEY-kuh-ring AHF-slui-tuhn fohr DEY-zuh HEWR-au-toh?

How much is the car per day?
Hoeveel kost de auto per dag?
Hoo-FEYL kohst duh AU-toh per dahg?

How many kilometers can I travel with this car?
Hoeveel kilometer kan ik reizen met deze auto?
Hoo-FEYL KEE-loh-mey-tuhr kahn ik RAI-zuhn met DEY-zuh AU-toh?

I would like maps of the region if you have them.
Ik zou graag kaarten van de regio willen hebben als je die hebt.
Ik zau grahg KAHR-tuhn fahn duh REY-gee-oh VI-luhn HE-buhn ahls yuh dee hebt.

When I am done with the car, where do I return it?
Als ik klaar ben met de auto, waar moet ik deze dan inleveren?
Ahls ik klahr ben met duh AU-toh, vahr moot ik DEY-zuh dahn IN-ley-vuh-ruhn?

Is this a standard or automatic transmission?
Is dit een schakelauto of een automaat?
Is dit uhn SGA-kuhl-au-toh ohf uhn au-toh-MAHT?

Is this car gas-efficient? How many kilometers per liter?
Is deze auto zuinig met benzine? Hoeveel kilometer per liter?
Is DEY-zuh AU-toh ZUI-nig met ben-ZEE-nuh? HOO-veyl KEE-loh-mey-tuhr per LEE-tuhr?

Where is the spare tire stored?
Waar wordt het reservewiel bewaard?
Vahr vohrdt het ruh-SER-vuh-veel buh-VAHRT?

Are there places around the city that are difficult to drive?
Zijn er plaatsen in de stad waar het moeilijk is om te rijden?
Sain er PLAHT-suhn in duh staht vahr het MOOEE-luhk is ohm tuh RAI-duhn?

At what time of the day is the traffic the worst?
Op welk tijdstip van de dag is het verkeer het drukst?
Ohp velk TAIT-stip fahn duh dahg is het fuhr-KEYR het druhkst?

We can't park right here.
We kunnen hier niet parkeren.
Vuh KUH-nuhn heer neet pahr-KEY-ruhn.

What is the speed limit?
Wat is de snelheidslimiet?
Vaht is duh SNEL-haits-lee-meet?

Keep the change.
Houd het wisselgeld.
Haut het VI-suhl-gelt.

Now let's get off here.
Laten we hier nu uitstappen.
LAH-tuhn vuh heer noo UIT-stah-puhn.

Where is the train station?
Waar is het treinstation?
Vahr is het TRAIN-stah-syohn?

Is the bus stop nearby?
Is de bushalte dichtbij?
Is duh BUHS-hahl-tuh digt-BAI?

When does the bus run?
Wanneer komt de bus?
Vah-NEYR kohmt duh buhs?

Where do I go to catch a taxi?
Waar moet ik heen om een taxi te nemen?
Vahr moot ik heyn ohm uhn TAHK-see tuh NEY-muhn?

Does the train go to the north station?
Gaat de trein naar station noord?
Gaht duh train nahr stah-SYON nohrt?

Where do I go to purchase tickets?
Waar kan ik kaartjes kopen?
Vahr kahn ik KAHR-tyuhs KOH-puhn?

How much is a ticket to the north?
Hoeveel kost een ticket naar het noorden?
HOO-feyl kohst uhn TI-kuht nahr het NOHR-duhn?

What is the next stop along this route?
Wat is de volgende halte op deze route?
Vaht is duh FOHL-guhn-duh HAHL-tuh ohp DEY-zuh ROO-tuh?

Can I have a ticket to the north?
Mag ik een ticket naar het noorden?
Mahg ik uhn TI-kuht nahr het NOHR-duhn?

Where is my designated platform?
Waar is mijn aangewezen perron?
Vahr is main AHN-guh-vey-zuhn per-OHN?

Where do I place my luggage?
Waar plaats ik mijn bagage?
Vahr plahts ik main bah-GAH-syuh?

Are there any planned closures today?
Zijn er sluitingen gepland voor vandaag?
Sain er SLUI-ting-uhn guh-PLEN fohr fahn-DAHG?

Where are the machines that dispense tickets?
Waar zijn de kaartjesautomaten?
Vahr sain duh KAHR-tyuhs-au-toh-mah-tuhn?

Does this car come with insurance?
Wordt deze auto met verzekering geleverd?
Vohrt DEY-zuh AU-toh met fuhr-ZEY-kuh-ring guh-LEY-fuhrt?

May I have a timetable, please?
Mag ik alstublieft een dienstregeling?
Mahg ik ahs-too-BLEEFT uhn DEENST-rey-guh-ling?

How often do trains come to this area?
Hoe vaak komen er treinen naar dit gebied?
Hoo fahk KOH-muhn er TRAI-nuhn nahr dit guh-BEET?

Is the train running late?
Is de trein vertraagd?
Is duh train fuhr-TRAHGT?

Has the train been cancelled?
Is de trein geannuleerd?
Is duh train guh-ah-noo-LEYRT?

Is this seat available?
Is deze stoel beschikbaar?
Is DEY-zuh stool buh-SGIK-bahr?

Do you mind if I sit here?
Vind je het goed als ik hier kom zitten?
Fint yuh het good ahls ik heer kohm ZI-tuhn?

I've lost my ticket.
Ik ben mijn ticket kwijt.
Ik ben main TI-kuht kvait.

Excuse me, this is my stop.
Pardon, dit is mijn halte.
Pahr-DOHN, dit is main HAHL-tuh.

Can you please open the window?
Kunt u alstublieft het raam openen?
Kuhnt oo ahs-too-BLEEFT het rahm OH-puh-nuhn?

Is smoking allowed in the car?
Is roken toegestaan in de auto?
Is ROH-kuhn TOO-guh-stahn in duh AU-toh?

Wait, my luggage is still on board!
Wacht, mijn bagage is nog aan boord!
Vahgt, main bah-GAH-syuh is nohg ahn bohrt!

Where can I get a map?
Waar kan ik een kaart krijgen?
Vahr kahn ik uhn kahrt KRAI-guhn?

What zone is this?
Welke zone is dit?
VEL-kuh ZOH-nuh is dit?

Please be careful of the gap!
Wees alsjeblieft voorzichtig met het gat!
Veys ahs-yuh-BLEEFT fohr-ZIG-tig met het gaht!

I am about to run out of gas.
Ik heb bijna geen benzine meer.
Ik heb BAI-nah geyn ben-ZEE-nuh meyr.

My tank is halfway full.
Mijn tank is halfvol.
Main tenk is HAHLF-fohl.

What type of gas does this car take?
Welke soort benzine gebruikt deze auto?
VEL-kuh sohrt ben-ZEE-nuh guh-BRUIKT DEY-zuh AU-toh?

There is gas leaking out of my car.
Er lekt benzine uit mijn auto.
Er lekt ben-ZEE-nuh uit main AU-toh.

Fill up the tank.
Vul de tank.
Fuhl duh tenk.

There is no more gas in my car.
Er zit geen benzine meer in mijn auto.
Er zit geyn ben-ZEE-nuh meyr in main AU-toh.

Where can I find the nearest gas station?
Waar vind ik het dichtstbijzijnde tankstation?
Vahr fint ik het DIGTST-bai-sain-duh TENK-stah-syohn?

The engine light for my car is on.
Het motorlampje voor mijn auto brandt.
Het MOH-tohr-lahmp-yuh fohr main AU-toh brahnt.

Do you mind if I drive?
Vind je het goed als ik rijd?
Fint yuh het goot ahls ik rait?

Please get in the back seat.
Ga alsjeblieft op de achterbank zitten.
Gah ahs-yuh-BLEEFT ohp duh AHG-tuhr-bahnk ZI-tuhn.

Let me get my bags out before you leave.
Laat me mijn koffers eruit pakken voordat je vertrekt.
Laht muh main KOH-fuhrs er-AUT PAH-kun FOHR-daht yuh fuhr-TREKT.

The weather is bad, please drive slowly.
Het weer is slecht, rijd u alstublieft langzaam.
Het veyr is slegt, rait oo ahs-too-BLEEFT LAHNG-zahm.

Our vehicle isn't equipped to travel there.
Ons voertuig is niet uitgerust om daarheen te reizen.
Ohns FOOR-tuig is neet UIT-guh-ruhst ohm dahr-HEYN tuh RAI-zuhn.

One ticket to the north, please.
Een kaartje naar het noorden, alstublieft.
Eyn KAHR-tyuh nahr het NOHR-duhn ahs-too-BLEEFT.

If you get lost, call me.
Als je verdwaalt, bel me dan.
Ahls yuh fuhr-DVAHLT, bel muh dahn.

That bus is overcrowded. I will wait for the next one.
Die bus is overvol. Ik wacht op de volgende.
Dee buhs is OH-fuhr-fohl. Ik wahgt ohp duh VOHL-guhn-duh.

Please, take my seat.
Neem mijn stoel alstublieft.
Neym main stool ahs-too-BLEEFT

Ma'am, I think your stop is coming up.
Mevrouw, ik denk dat uw halte eraan komt.
Muh-FRAU, ik denk daht ew HAHL-tuh er-AHN kohmt.

Wake me up when we get to our destination.
Maak me wakker als we op onze bestemming aankomen.
Mahk muh VAH-kuhr ahls vuh ohp OHN-zuh buh-STE-ming AHN-koh-muhn.

I would like to purchase a travel pass for the entire day.
Ik wil een reispas kopen voor de hele dag.
Ik vil un RAIS-pahs KOH-puhn fohr duh HEY-luh dahg.

Would you like to swap seats with me?
Wil je met mij van stoel wisselen?
Vil yuh met mai fahn stool VI-suh-luhn?

I want to sit with my family.
Ik wil bij mijn familie zitten.
Ik vil bai main fah-MEE-lee ZI-tuhn.

I would like a window seat for this trip.
Ik wil graag een stoel bij het raam voor deze reis.
Ik vil grahg uhn stool bai het rahm fohr DEY-zuh rais.

RELIGIOUS QUESTIONS

Where can I go to pray?
Waar kan ik heen om te bidden?
Vahr kahn ik heyn ohm tuh BI-duhn?

What services does your church offer?
Welke diensten biedt uw kerk aan?
VEL-kuh DEEN-stuhn beet ew kerk ahn?

Are you non-denominational?
Bent u niet-confessioneel?
Bent oo neet kohn-FE-syoh-neyl?

Is there a shuttle to your church?
Is er een shuttle naar uw kerk?
Is er uhn SYU-tuhl nahr ew kerk?

How long does church last?
Hoe lang duurt de kerkdienst?
Hoo lahng duhrt duh kerk-DEENST?

Where is your bathroom?
Waar is het toilet?
Vahr is heht twah-LET?

What should I wear to your services?
Wat moet ik dragen voor uw diensten?
Vaht moot ik DRAH-guhn fohr ew DEEN-stuhn?

Where is the nearest Catholic church?
Waar is de dichtstbijzijnde katholieke kerk?
Vahr is duh DIGTST-bai-sain-duh kah-toh-LEE-kuh kerk?

Where is the nearest mosque?
Waar is de dichtstbijzijnde moskee?
Vahr is duh DIGTST-bai-sain-duh mohs-KEY?

Does your church perform weddings?
Voert uw kerk bruiloften uit?
Foort ew kerk BRUI-lohf-tuhn uit?

Who is getting married?
Wie gaat er trouwen?
Vee gaht er TRAU-vuhn?

Will our marriage license be legal if we leave the country?
Is onze huwelijksvergunning legaal als we het land verlaten?
Is OHN-zuh HOO-vuh-luhks fuhr-GUH-ning luh-GAHL ahls vuh het lahnt fuhr-LAH-tuhn?

Where do we get our marriage license?
Waar halen we onze huwelijksvergunning?
Vahr HAH-luhn vuh OHN-zuh HOO-vuh-luks fuhr-GUH-ning?

What is the charge for marrying us?
Wat kost het om te trouwen?
Vaht kohst het ohm tuh TRAU-vuhn?

Do you handle same-sex marriages?
Voeren jullie ook homohuwelijken uit?
FOO-ruhn YUH-lee ohk HOH-moh-hoo-vuh-luh-kuhn uit?

Please gather here to pray.
Kom alstublieft hier bijeen om te bidden.
Kohm ahs-too-BLEEFT heer bai-EYN ohm tuh BI-duhn.

I would like to lead a sermon.
Ik zou graag een preek willen houden.
Ik zau grahg uhn preyk VI-luhn HAU-duhn.

I would like to help with prayer.
Ik zou graag willen helpen met een gebed.
Ik zau grahg VI-luhn HEL-puhn met uhn guh-BED.

How should I dress before arriving?
Hoe moet ik me kleden voordat ik aankom?
Hoo moot ik muh KLEY-duhn FOHR-daht ik AHN-kohm?

What are your rules?
Wat zijn jullie regels?
Vaht sain YUH-lee REY-guhls?

Are cell phones allowed in your building?
Zijn mobiele telefoons toegestaan in uw gebouw?
Sain moh-BEE-luh tey-luh-FOHNS TOO-guh-stahn in ew guh-BAUW?

I plan on bringing my family this Sunday.
Ik ben van plan mijn gezin deze zondag mee te nemen.
Ik ben fahn plahn main guh-ZIN DEY-zuh ZOHN-dahg mey tuh NEY-muhn.

Do you accept donations?
Accepteert u donaties?
Ak-sep-TEYRT oo doh-NAHT-sees?

I would like to offer my time to your cause.
Ik zou graag mijn tijd willen geven aan uw geloof.
Ik zau grahg main tait VI-luhn GEY-fuhn ahn ew guh-LOHF.

What book should I be reading from?
Uit welk boek moet ik lezen?
Uit velk book moot ik LEY-zuhn?

Do you have a gift store?
Hebben jullie een cadeauwinkel?
HEB-uhn YUH-lee uhn kah-DOH-wing-kuhl?

EMERGENCY

I need help over here!
Ik heb hier hulp nodig!
Ik heb heer huhlp NOH-duhg!

I'm lost, please help me.
Ik ben verdwaald, help me alstublieft.
Ik ben fuhr-DVAHLT, help muh ahs-too-BLEEFT.

Someone call the police!
Iemand bel de politie!
EE-mahnt bel duh poh-LEET-see!

Is there a lawyer who speaks English?
Is er een advocaat die Engels spreekt?
Is er uhn aht-foh-KAHT dee ENG-uhls spreykt?

Please help, my car doesn't work.
Help alstublieft, mijn auto doet het niet.
Help ahs-too-BLEEFT, main AU-toh doot het neet.

There was a collision!
Er was een botsing!
Er vahs uhn BOHT-sing.

Call an ambulance!
Bel een ambulance!
Bel uhn ahm-boo-LAHN-suh.

Am I under arrest?
Ben ik gearresteerd?
Ben ik guh-ah-res-TEYRT?

I need an interpreter, this is an emergency!
Ik heb een tolk nodig, dit is een noodgeval!
Ik heb uhn tohlk NOH-dug, dit is uhn NOHT-guh-fahl!

My back hurts.
Mijn rug doet pijn.
Main ruhg doot pain.

Is there an American consulate here?
Is hier een Amerikaans consulaat?
Is heer uhn ah-mey-ree-KAHNS kohn-soo-LAHT?

I'm sick and don't feel too well.
Ik ben ziek en voel me niet zo lekker.
Ik ben zeek en fool muh neet zoh LE-kuhr.

Is there a pharmacy where I can get medicine?
Is er een apotheek waar ik medicijnen kan krijgen?
Is er uhn ah-poh-TEYK vahr ik mey-dee-SAI-nuhn kahn KRAI-guhn?

I need a doctor immediately.
Ik heb onmiddellijk een dokter nodig.
Ik heb ohn-MI-duh-luhk uhn DOHK-tuhr NOH-duhg.

I have a tooth missing.
Ik mis een tand.
Ik mis uhn tahnt.

Please! Someone bring my child to me!
Alstublieft! Iemand, breng mijn kind naar mij!
Ahs-too-BLEEFT! EE-mahnt breng main kint nahr mai!

Where does it hurt?
Waar doet het pijn?
Vahr doot het pain?

Hold on to me!
Hou me vast!
Hau muh fahst!

There's an emergency!
Er is een noodgeval!
Er is uhn NOHT-guh-fahl.

I need a telephone to call for help.
Ik heb een telefoon nodig om hulp te roepen.
Ik heb uhn tey-luh-FOHN NOH-dug ohm huhlp tuh ROO-puhn.

80

My nose is bleeding.
Mijn neus bloedt.
Main nuhs bloot.

I twisted my ankle.
Ik verdraaide mijn enkel.
Ik fuhr-DRIE-duh main ENG-kuhl.

I don't feel so good.
Ik voel me niet zo goed.
Ik fool muh neet goot.

Don't move, please.
Beweeg niet, alstublieft.
Buh-VEYG neet ahs-too-BLEEFT.

Hello operator, can I place a collect call?
Hallo telefoniste, kan ik een collect call plaatsen?
HAH-loh tey-luh-foh-NI-stuh, kahn ik uhn koh-LEKT kahl PLAHT-suhn?

I'll get a doctor for you.
Ik zal een dokter voor je halen.
Ik zahl uhn DOK-tuhr fohr yuh HAH-luhn.

Please hold my passports for a while.
Bewaar mijn paspoorten een tijdje.
Buh-VAHR main PAHS-pohrt uhn TAIT-yuh.

I lost my wallet.
Ik ben mijn portemonnee kwijt.
Ik ben main por-tuh-moh-NEY kvait.

I have a condition! Please check my wallet.
Ik heb een aandoening! Controleer mijn portemonnee alstublieft.
Ik heb uhn AHN-doo-ning! Kohn-troh-LEYR main pohr-tuh-moh-NEY ahs-too-BLEEFT.

My wife is in labor, please help!
Mijn vrouw heeft weeën, help alstublieft!
Main frau heyft WEY-uhn, help ahs-too-BLEEFT!

I would like to talk to my lawyer.
Ik wil graag met mijn advocaat praten.
Ik vil grahg met main aht-foh-KAHT PRAH-tuhn.

81

It's an earthquake!
Het is een aardbeving!
Het is uhn AHRT-bey-ving!

Get under the desk and protect your head.
Ga onder het bureau zitten en bescherm je hoofd.
Gah OHN-duhr het boo-ROH ZI-tuhn en buh-SGERM yuh hohft.

How can I help you?
Hoe kan ik u helpen?
Hoo kahn ik oo HEL-puhn?

Everyone, he needs help!
Iedereen, hij heeft hulp nodig!
Ee-duh-REYN, hai heyft huhlp NOH-dug!

Yes, help me get an ambulance.
Ja, help me een ambulance te halen.
Yah, help muh uhn ahm-boo-LAHN-suh tuh HAH-luhn.

Thank you, but I am fine. Please don't help me.
Bedankt, maar het gaat goed. Help me alstublieft niet.
Buh-DAHNKT, mahr het gaht goot. Help muh ahs-too-BLEEFT neet.

I need help carrying this injured person.
Ik heb hulp nodig bij het dragen van deze gewonde.
Ik heb huhlp NOH-duhg bai het DRAH-guhn fahn DEY-zuh guh-WOHN-duh.

TECHNOLOGY

What is the country's official website?
Wat is de officiële website van het land?
Vaht is duh oh-fee-SHEY-luh WEB-siet fahn het lahnt?

Do you know the name of a good wi-fi café?
Kent u de naam van een goed café met wifi?
Kent oo duh nahm fahn uhn goot kah-FEY met VEE-fee?

Do you have any experience with computers?
Heb je ervaring met computers?
Heb yuh er-VAH-ring met kohm-PYOO-tuhrs?

How well do you know Apple products?
Hoe goed ken je de Apple-producten?
Hoo goot ken yuh duh Apple proh-DUHK-tuhn?

What kind of work did you do with computers?
Wat voor werk heb je met computers gedaan?
Vaht fohr verk heb yuh met kohm-PYOO-tuhrs guh-DAHN?

Are you a programmer?
Ben je een programmeur?
Ben yuh uhn proh-grah-MUHR?

Are you a developer?
Ben jij een ontwikkelaar?
Ben yai uhn ohnt-VI-kuh-lahr?

I want to use this computer instead of that one.
Ik wil deze computer gebruiken in plaats van die.
Ik vil DEY-zuh kohm-PYOO-tuhr guh-BRUI-kuhn in plahts fahn dee.

Do you know where I can buy discount computer parts?
Weet je waar ik afgeprijsde computeronderdelen kan kopen?
Veyt yuh vahr ik ahf-guh-PRAIS-duh kohm-PYOO-tuhr-ohn-duhr-dey-luhn kahn KOH-puhn?

I have ten years of experience with Windows.
Ik heb tien jaar ervaring met Windows.
Ik heb teen yahr er-FAH-ring met VIN-dohs.

What is the wi-fi password?
Wat is het wifi-wachtwoord?
Vaht is het VEE-fee VAHGT-vohrt?

I need to have my login information reset.
Ik moet mijn inloggegevens laten resetten.
Ik moot main IN-lohg-guh-gey-vuns LAH-tuhn ree-SE-tuhn.

The hard drive is making a clicking noise.
De harde schijf maakt een klikgeluid.
Duh HAHR-duh sgaif mahkt uhn KLIK-guh-luit.

How do I uninstall this program from my device?
Hoe verwijder ik dit programma van mijn apparaat?
Hoo fuhr-VAI-duhr ik dit proh-GRAH-mah fahn main ah-pah-RAHT?

Can you help me set up a new account with this website?
Kunt u mij helpen bij het opzetten van een nieuw account op deze website?
Kuhnt oo mai HEL-puhn bai het OHP-ze-tuhn fahn uhn neew ah-KAUNT ohp DEY-zuh WEB-siet?

Why is the internet so slow?
Waarom is het internet zo traag?
Vah-ROHM is het IN-tuhr-net zoh trahg?

Why is YouTube buffering every video I play?
Waarom buffert YouTube elke video die ik afspeel?
Vah-ROHM BUH-fuhrt YouTube EL-kuh VEE-dee-oh dee ik AHF-speyl?

My web camera isn't displaying a picture.
Mijn web camera geeft geen afbeelding weer.
Main veb KAH-muh-rah geyft geyn AHF-beyl-ding weyr.

I have no bars on my phone.
Ik heb geen bereik op mijn telefoon.
Ik heb geyn BUH-raik ohp main tey-luh-FOHN.

Where can I get my phone serviced?

Waar kan ik mijn telefoon laten nakijken?

Vahr kahn ik main tey-luh-FOHN LAH-tuhn NAH-kai-kuhn?

My phone shows that it is charging but won't charge.

Mijn telefoon zegt dat hij oplaadt, maar hij laadt niet op.

Main tey-luh-FOHN zegt daht hai OHP-laht mahr hai laht neet ohp.

I think someone else is controlling my computer.

Ik denk dat iemand anders mijn computer bedient.

Ik denk daht IE-mahnt AHN-duhrs main kohm-PYOO-tuhr buh-DEENT.

My computer just gave a blue screen and shut down.

Mijn computer gaf zojuist een blauw scherm en ging uit.

Main kohm-PYOO-tuhr gahf zoh-YUIST uhn blauw sgerm en ging uit.

Do you have the battery for this laptop?

Heeft u de batterij voor deze laptop?

Heyft oo duh bah-tuh-RAI fohr DEY-zuh LAP-tohp.

Where can I get a compatible adapter?

Waar kan ik een compatibele adapter krijgen?

Vahr kahn ik uhn kohm-pah-TEE-buh-luh ah-DAHP-tuhr KRAI-guhn?

I can't get online with the information you gave me.

Ik kan niet online komen met de informatie die je me hebt gegeven.

Ik kahn neet ohn-LIEN KOH-muhn met duh in-fohr-MAHT-see dee yuh muh hebt guh-GEY-fuhn.

This keyboard is not working correctly.

Dit toetsenbord werkt niet correct.

Dit TOOT-suhn-bohrt werkt neet koh-REKT.

What is the login information for this computer?

Wat zijn de inloggegevens voor deze computer?

Vaht zijn duh IN-long-guh-gey-fuhns fohr DEY-zuh kohm-PYOO-tuhr?

I need you to update my computer.

Ik wil dat je mijn computer bijwerkt.

Ik vil daht yuh main kohm-PYOO-tuhr BAI-verkt.

Can you build my website?

Kan je mijn website bouwen?

Kahn yuh main WEB-siet BAU-vuhn?

I prefer Wordpress.
Ik geef de voorkeur aan Wordpress.
Ik geyf duh FOHR-kuhr ahn WORD-press.

What are your rates per hour?
Wat is uw uurtarief?
Vaht is ew oor-tah-REEF?

Do you have experience handling email servers?
Heb je ervaring met e-mailservers?
Heb yuh er-FAH-ring met EE-meyl-suhr-vuhrs?

I am locked out of my account, can you help?
Ik heb geen toegang tot mijn account, kunt u helpen?
Ik heb geyn TOO-gahng toht main ah-KAUNT, kuhnt oo HEL-puhn?

None of the emails I am sending are going through.
Geen enkele e-mail die ik verstuur komt erdoor.
Geyn ENG-kuh-luh e-mail dee ik fer-STUHR KOHMT er-DOHR.

The time and date on my computer are wrong.
De tijd en datum op mijn computer kloppen niet.
Duh tait en DAH-tuhm ohp main kohm-PYOO-tuhr KLOH-puhn neet.

Is this game free to play?
Is dit spel gratis om te spelen?
Is dit spel GRAH-tis ohm tuh SPEY-luhn?

Where do I go to download the client?
Waar moet ik zijn om de client te downloaden?
Vahr moet ik sain ohm duh klai-YENT tuh DAUN-loh-duhn?

I am having troubles chatting with my family.
Ik heb problemen met het chatten met mijn familie.
Ik heb proh-BLEY-muhn met het CHE-tuhn met main fah-MEE-lee.

Is this the fastest computer here?
Is dit de snelste computer hier?
Is dit duh SNELS-tuh kohm-PYOO-tuhr heer?

How much space is on the computer?
Hoeveel ruimte heeft de computer?
HOO-feyl RUIM-tuh heyft duh kohm-PYOO-tuhr?

Will my profile be deleted once I log out? Or does it save?

Wordt mijn profiel verwijderd zodra ik uitlog? Of wordt het bewaard?

Vohrt main proh-FEEL fuhr-VAI-duhrt zoh-DRAH ik UIT-lohg? Of vohrt het buh-VAHRT?

How much do you charge for computer use?

Hoeveel rekent u voor het gebruik van de computer?

HOO-feyl REY-kuhnt oo fohr het guh-BRUIK fahn duh kohm-PYOO-tuhr?

Are group discounts offered?

Worden er groepskortingen aangeboden?

VOHR-duhn er GROOPS-kohr-ting-uhn AHN-guh-boh-duhn?

Can I use my own headphones with your computer?

Kan ik mijn eigen koptelefoon gebruiken met uw computer?

Kahn ik main AI-guhn KOHP-tey-luh-fohn guh-BRUI-kuhn met ew kohm-PYOO-tuhr?

Do you have a data cap?

Is er een datalimiet?

Is er uhn DAH-tah-lee-meet?

I think this computer has a virus.

Ik denk dat deze computer een virus heeft.

Ik denk daht DEY-zuh kohm-PYOO-tuhr uhn VEE-ruhs heyft.

The battery for my laptop is running low.

De batterij van mijn laptop is bijna leeg.

Duh bah-tuh-RAI fahn main LAP-top is BAI-nah leyg.

Where can I plug this in? I need to recharge my device.

Waar kan ik dit aansluiten? Ik moet mijn apparaat opladen.

Vahr kahn ik dit AHN-slui-tuhn? Ik moot main ah-pah-RAHT OHP-lah-duhn.

Do you have a mini-USB cord?

Heb je een mini-USB-kabel?

Heb yuh uhn MEE-nee oo-es-BEY KAH-buhl?

Where can I go to watch the game?

Waar kan ik naar de wedstrijd kijken?

Vahr kahn ik nahr duh VET-strait KAI-kuhn?

Do you have an iPhone charger?
Heb je een iPhone-oplader?
Heb yuh uhn iPhone OHP-lah-duhr?

I need a new battery for my watch.
Ik heb een nieuwe batterij nodig voor mijn horloge.
Ik heb uhn NEE-vuh bah-tuh-RAI NOH-duhg fohr main hohr-LOH-syuh.

I need to borrow an HDMI cord.
Ik moet een HDMI-kabel lenen.
Ik moot uhn hah-dey-em-EE KAH-buhl LEY-nuhn.

What happens when I exceed the data cap?
Wat gebeurt er als ik de datalimiet overschrijd?
Vaht guh-BUHRT er ahls ik duh DAH-tah-lee-meet oh-fuhr-SGRAIT?

Can you help me pair my Bluetooth device?
Kunt u mij helpen mijn Bluetooth-apparaat te koppelen?
Kuhnt oo mai HEL-puhn main Bluetooth ah-pah-RAHT tuh KOH-puh-luhn?

I need a longer ethernet cord.
Ik heb een langere ethernetkabel nodig.
Ik heb uhn LAHNG-uh-ruh EY-tuhr-net-kah-buhl NOH-duhg.

Why is this website restricted?
Waarom is deze website beperkt?
VAH-rohm is DEY-zuh WEB-siet buh-PERKT?

How can I unblock this website?
Hoe kan ik deze website deblokkeren?
Hoo kahn ik DEY-zuh WEB-siet dey-bloh-KEY-ruhn?

Is that television 4k or higher?
Is die televisie 4K of hoger?
Is DEE tey-luh-FEE-see feer-KAH ohf HOH-guhr?

Do you have the Office suite on this computer?
Heeft u het Office-pakket op deze computer?
Heyft oo het OH-fis-pah-ket ohp DEY-zuh kohm-PYOO-tuhr?

This application won't install on my device.
Deze applicatie kan niet op mijn apparaat worden geïnstalleerd.
DEY-zuh ah-plee-KAHT-see kahn neet ohp main ah-pah-RAHT VOHR-duhn guh-IN-stah-leyrt.

Can you change the channel on the television?
Kun je het kanaal op de televisie wijzigen?
Kun yuh het kah-NAHL ohp duh tey-luh-FEE-see VAI-zuh-gun?

I think a fuse blew.
Ik geloof dat er een zekering is gesprongen.
Ik guh-LOHF daht er uhn ZEY-kuh-ring is guh-SPROHNG-uhnn.

The screen is black and won't come on.
Het scherm is zwart en gaat niet aan.
Het sgerm is zvahrt en gaht neet ahn.

I keep getting pop-ups on every website.
Ik krijg steeds pop-ups op elke website.
Ik kraig steyts POHP-uhps ohp EL-kuh WEB-siet.

This computer is moving much slower than it should.
Deze computer werkt veel langzamer dan zou moeten.
DEY-zuh kohm-PYOO-tuhr werkt feyl LAHNG-zah-muhr dahn zau MOO-tuhn.

I need to reactivate my copy of Windows.
Ik moet mijn exemplaar van Windows opnieuw activeren.
Ik moot main ek-sem-PLAHR fahn WIN-dows op-NEEW ahk-tee-FEY-ruhn.

Why is this website blocked on my laptop?
Waarom is deze website op mijn laptop geblokkeerd?
VAH-rohm is DEY-zuh WEB-siet ohp main LAP-top guh-bloh-KEYRT?

Can you show me how to download videos to my computer?
Kun je me laten zien hoe ik video's op mijn computer kan downloaden?
Kuhn yuh muh LAH-tuhn zeen hoo ik VEE-dee-oos ohp main kohm-PYOO-tuhr kahn DOWN-loa-den?

Can I insert a flash drive into this computer?
Kan ik een USB-stick in deze computer plaatsen?
Kahn ik uhn oo-es-BEY-stick in DEY-zuh kohm-PYOO-tuhr PLAHT-suhn?

I want to change computers.
Ik wil van computer wisselen.
Ik vil fahn kohm-PYOO-tuhr VI-suh-luhn.

Is Chrome the only browser I can use with this computer?

Is Chrome de enige browser die ik met deze computer kan gebruiken?

Is Chrome duh EY-nuh-guh BROW-suhr dee ik met DEY-zuh kohm-PYOO-tuhr kahn guh-BRUI-kuhn?

Do you track my usage on any of these devices?

Houdt u mijn gebruik bij op een van deze apparaten?

Haut oo main guh-BRUIK bai ohp eyn fahn DEY-zuh ah-pah-RAH-tuhn?

CONVERSATION TIPS

Pardon me.
Sorry.
SOH-ree.

Please speak more slowly.
Spreek alstublieft langzamer.
Spreyk ahs-too-BLEEFT LAHNG-zah-muhr.

I don't understand.
Ik begrijp het niet.
Ik buh-GRAIP het neet.

Can you say that more clearly?
Kunt u dat duidelijker zeggen?
Kuhnt oo daht DUI-duh-luh-kuhr ZE-guhn?

I don't speak Spanish very well.
Ik spreek niet zo goed Spaans.
Ik spreyk neet zoh goot spahns.

Can you please translate that to English for me?
Kunt u dat alstublieft voor mij naar het Engels vertalen?
Kuhnt oo daht ahs-too-BLEEFT fohr mai nahr het ENG-uhls fuhr-TAH-luhn?

Let's talk over there where it is quieter.
Laten we daar praten waar het rustiger is.
LAH-tuhn vuh dahr PRAH-tuhn vahr het RUH-sti-guhr is.

Sit down over there.
Ga daar zitten.
Gah dahr ZI-tuhn.

May I?
Mag ik?
Mahg ik?

I am from America.
Ik kom uit Amerika.
Ik kohm uit ah-MEY-ree-kah.

Am I talking too much?
Praat ik te veel?
Praht ik tuh feyl?

I speak your language badly.
Ik spreek uw taal slecht.
Ik spreyk ew tahl slegt.

Am I saying that word correctly?
Zeg ik dat woord correct?
Zeg ik daht vohrt koh-REKT?

You speak English very well.
Je spreekt erg goed Engels.
Yuh spreykt erg goot ENG-uhls.

This is my first time in your lovely country.
Dit is mijn eerste keer in je mooie land.
Dit is main EYR-stuh keyr in yuh MOH-yuh lahnt.

Write that information down on this piece of paper.
Schrijf die informatie op dit vel papier.
Sgraif dee in-fohr-MAHT-see ohp dit fel pah-PEER.

Do you understand?
Begrijp je?
Buh-GRAIP yuh?

How do you pronounce that word?
Hoe spreek je dat woord uit?
Hoo spreyk yuh daht vohrt uit?

Is this how you write this word?
Schrijf je dit woord zo?
Sgraif yuh dit vohrt zoh?

Can you give me an example?
Kun je me een voorbeeld geven?
Kuhn yuh muh uhn FOHR-beylt GEY-vuhn?

Wait a moment, please.

Wacht even, alstublieft.

Vahgt EY-fuhn, ahs-too-BLEEFT.

If there is anything you want, tell me.

Zeg het maar als er iets is wat je wilt.

Zeg het mahr ahls er eets is vaht yuh vilt.

I don't want to bother you anymore, so I will go.

Ik wil je niet meer lastig vallen, dus ik ga.

Ik vil yuh neet meyr LAH-stug FAH-luhn, duhs ik gah.

Please take care of yourself.

Zorg alsjeblieft voor jezelf.

Zohrg ahs-yuh-BLEEFT fohr yuh-ZELF.

When you arrive, let us know.

Laat het ons weten wanneer je aankomt.

Laht het ohns VEY-tuhn vah-NEYR yuh AHN-kohmt.

DATE NIGHT

What is your telephone number?
Wat is je telefoonnummer?
Vaht is yuh tey-luh-FOHN-nuh-muhr?

I'll call you for the next date.
Ik bel je voor de volgende date.
Ik bel yuh fohr duh FOHL-guhn-duh deyt.

I had a good time, can't wait to see you again.
Ik heb het leuk gehad, ik kan niet wachten om je weer te zien.
Ik heb het luhk guh-HAHT, ik kahn neet VAHG-tuhn ohm yuh veyr tuh zeen.

I'll pay for dinner tonight.
Ik betaal vanavond voor het eten.
Ik buh-TAHL fahn-AH-fohnt fohr het EY-tuhn.

Dinner at my place?
Etentje bij mij thuis?
EY-tuhn-tyuh bai mai tuis?

I don't think we should see each other anymore.
Ik denk dat we elkaar niet meer moeten zien.
Ik denk daht vuh el-KAHR neet meyr MOO-tuhn zeen.

I'm afraid this will be the last time we see each other.
Ik ben bang dat dit de laatste keer is dat we elkaar zien.
Ik ben bahng daht dit duh LAHT-stuh keyr is daht vuh el-KAHR zeen.

You look fantastic.
Je ziet er fantastisch uit.
Yuh zeet er fahn-TAHS-tees uit.

Would you like to dance with me?
Wil je met me dansen?
Vil yuh met muh DAHN-suhn?

Are there any 3D cinemas in this city?
Zijn er 3D-bioscopen in deze stad?
Sain er dree-DEY bee-ohs-KOH-puhn in DEY-zuh staht?

We should walk along the beach.
We moeten langs het strand lopen.
Vuh MOO-tuhn lahngs het strahnt LOH-puhn.

I hope you like my car.
Ik hoop dat je mijn auto mooi vindt.
Ik hohp daht yuh main AU-toh mohee fint.

What movies are playing today?
Welke films draaien er vandaag?
VEL-kuh films DRIE-uhn er fahn-DAHG?

I've seen this film, but I wouldn't mind watching it again.
Ik heb deze film gezien, maar ik zou het niet erg vinden om hem nog een
keer te bekijken.
*Ik heb DEY-zuh guh-ZEEN, mahr ik zau het neet erg FIN-duhn ohm hem
nohg uhnn keer tuh buh-KAI-kuhn.*

Do you know how to dance salsa?
Kan jij salsadansen?
Kahn yai SAHL-sah-dahn-suhn?

We can dance all night.
We kunnen de hele nacht dansen.
Vuh KUH-nuhn duh HEY-luh nahgt DAHN-suhn.

I have some friends that will be joining us tonight.
Ik heb een paar vrienden die vanavond bij ons komen.
Ik heb uhn pahr FREEN-duhn dee fahn-AH-fohnt bai ohns KOH-muhn.

Is this a musical or a regular concert?
Is dit een musical of een gewoon concert?
Is dit uhn MYOO-si-kahl ohf uhn guh-VOHN kohn-SERT?

Did you get VIP tickets?
Heb je VIP-tickets gekregen?
Heb yuh vee-ie-PEE TI-kuhts guh-KREY-guhn?

I'm going to have to cancel on you tonight. Maybe another time?
Ik moet je vanavond afzeggen. Misschien een andere keer?
Ik moot yuh fahn-AH-fohnt AHF-ze-guhn. Mis-GEEN uhn AHN-duh-ruh keyr?

If you want, we can go to your place.
Als je wilt, kunnen we naar jouw huis gaan.
Ahls yuh vilt, KUH-nuhn vuh nahr yau huis gahn.

I'll pick you up tonight.
Ik haal je vanavond op.
Ik hahl yuh fahn-AH-fohnt ohp.

This one is for you!
Deze is voor jou!
DEY-zuh is fohr yau!

What time does the party start?
Hoe laat begint het feest?
Hoo laht buh-GINT het feyst?

Will it end on time or will you have to leave early?
Is het op tijd afgelopen of moet je vroeg vertrekken?
Is het ohp tait ahf-ge-LOH-puhn ohf moot yuh froog fuhr-TRE-kuhn?

Did you like your gift?
Vond je je cadeau leuk?
Fohnt yuh yuh kah-DOH luhk?

I want to invite you to watch a movie with me tonight.
Ik wil je uitnodigen om vanavond een film met mij te kijken.
Ik vil yuh UIT-noh-duh-guhn ohm fahn-AH-fohnt uhn film met mai tuh KAI-kuhn.

Do you want anything to drink?
Wil je iets drinken?
Vil yuh eets DRING-kuhn?

I am twenty-six years old.
Ik ben zesentwintig jaar oud.
Ik ben zes-en-TVIN-tig yahr aut.

You're invited to a small party I'm having at my house.
Je bent uitgenodigd voor een klein feestje bij mij thuis.
Yuh bent UIT-guh-noh-duhgt fohr uhn klain FEYST-yuh bai mai tuis.

I love you.
Ik hou van jou.
Ik hau fahn yau.

We should go to the arcade.
We moeten naar de speelhal gaan.
Vuh MOO-tuhn nahr duh SPEYL-hahl gahn.

Have you ever played this game before?
Heb je dit spel ooit eerder gespeeld?
Heb yuh dit spel oheet EYR-duhr guh-SPEYLT?

Going on this ferry would be really romantic.
Met deze veerboot meegaan zou echt romantisch zijn.
Met DEY-zuh FEYR-boot meh-gahn zau egt roh-MAHN-tees sain.

How about a candlelight dinner?
Wat denk je van een diner bij kaarslicht?
Vaht denk yuh fahn uhn dee-NEY bai KAHRS-ligt?

Let's dance and sing!
Laten we dansen en zingen!
LAH-tuhn vuh DAHN-suhn en ZING-uhn!

Will you marry me?
Wil je met me trouwen?
Vil yuh met muh TRAU-vuhn?

Set the table, please.
Dek de tafel alsjeblieft.
Dek duh TAH-fuhl ahs-yuh-BLEEFT.

Here are the dishes and the glasses.
Hier zijn de borden en de glazen.
Heer sain duh BOHR-duhn en duh GLAH-zuhn.

Where is the cutlery?
Waar is het bestek?
Vahr is het buh-STEK?

May I hold your hand?
Mag ik je hand vasthouden?
Mahg ik yuh hahnt VAHST-hau-duhn?

Let me get that for you.
Laat mij dat voor je pakken.
Laht mai daht fohr yuh PAHK-uhn.

I think our song is playing!
Ik geloof dat ons liedje speelt!
Ik guh-LOHF daht ohns LEET-yuh speylt!

Let's make a wish together.
Laten we samen een wens doen.
LAH-tuhn vuh SAH-muhn uhn vens doon.

Is there anything that you want from me?
Is er iets wat je van me wilt?
Is er eets vaht yuh fahn muh vilt?

There is nowhere I would rather be than right here with you.
Ik zou nergens liever zijn dan hier bij jou.
Ik zau NER-guhns LEE-fuhr sain dahn heer bai yau.

I'll give you a ride back to your place.
Ik geef je een lift terug naar je huis.
Ik geyf yuh uhn lift tuh-ruhg naar yuh huis.

Would you like me to hold your purse?
Wil je dat ik je tas vasthoud?
Vil yuh daht ik yuh tahs FAHST-haut?

Let's pray before we eat our meal.
Laten we bidden voordat we onze maaltijd eten.
LAH-tuhn vuh BI-duhn FOHR-dat vuh OHN-zuh MAHL-tait EY-tuhn.

Do you need a napkin?
Heb je een servet nodig?
Heb yuh uhn ser-FET NOH-duhg?

I'm thirsty.
Ik heb dorst.
Ik heb dohrst.

I hope you enjoy your meal.
Ik hoop dat je van je maaltijd geniet.
Ik hohp daht yuh fahn yuh MAHL-tait guh-NEET.

I need to add more salt to the salt shaker.
Ik moet meer zout in het zoutvaatje doen.
Ik moot meyr zaut in het ZAUT-faht-yuh doon.

We should get married!
Laten we trouwen!
LAH-tuhn vuh TRAU-vuhn!

How old are you?
Hoe oud ben je?
Hoo aut ben yuh?

Will you dream of me?
Droom jij over mij?
Drohm yai OH-fuhr mai?

Thank you very much for the wonderful date last night.
Heel erg bedankt voor de geweldige date van gisteravond.
Heyl erg buh-DAHNKT fohr duh guh-VEL-duh-guh deyt fahn gis-tuhr-AH-fohnt.

Would you like to come to a party this weekend?
Heb je zin om dit weekend naar een feestje te gaan?
Heb juh zin ohm dit WEE-kent nahr uhn FEYST-yuh tuh gahn?

This Saturday night, right?
Deze zaterdagavond, toch?
DEY-zuh ZAH-tuhr-dahg AH-fohnt, tohg?

I will be lonely without you.
Ik zal eenzaam zijn zonder jou.
Ik zahl EYN-zahm sain ZOHN-duhr yau.

Please stay the night?
Blijf je slapen, alsjeblieft?
Blaif yuh SLAH-puhn, ahs-yuh-BLEEFT?

I like your fragrance.
Ik hou van je geurtje.
Ik hau fahn yuh GUHR-tyuh.

That is a beautiful outfit you're wearing.
Dat is een mooie outfit die je draagt.
Daht is uhn MOH-yuh AUT-fit dee yuh drahgt.

You look beautiful.
Je ziet er heel mooi uit.
Yuh zeet er heyl mohee uit.

Let me help you out of the car.
Laat me je uit de auto helpen.
Laht muh yuh uit duh AU-toh HEL-puhn.

Sarah, will you come with me to dinner?
Sarah, wil je met mij mee uit eten?
SAH-rah, vil yuh met mai mee uit EY-tuhn?

I would like to ask you out on a date.
Ik zou je graag mee willen vragen op een date.
Ik zau yuh grahg uit WIL-uhn FRAH-guhn ohp uhn date.

Are you free tonight?
Ben je vrij vanavond?
Ben yuh frai fahn-AH-fohnt?

This is my phone number. Call me anytime.
Dit is mijn telefoonnummer. Je kunt me altijd bellen.
Dit is main tey-luh-FOHN-nuh-muhr. Yuh kuhnt muh AHL-tait BE-luhn.

Can I hug you?
Mag ik je omhelzen?
Mahg ik yuh ohm-HEL-zuhn?

Would you like to sing karaoke?
Wil je karaoke zingen?
Vil yuh kah-rah-OH-kuh ZING-uhn?

What kind of song would you like to sing?
Wat voor soort liedje wil je zingen?
Vaht fohr sohrt LEET-yuh vil yuh ZING-uhn?

Have you ever sung this song before?
Heb je dit liedje ooit eerder gezongen?
Heb yuh dit leet-yuh oheet EYR-duhr guh-ZOHNG-uhn?

We can sing it together.
We kunnen het samen zingen.
Vuh KUH-nuhn het SAH-muhn ZING-uhn.

Can I kiss you?
Mag ik je kussen?
Mahg ik yuh KUH-suhn?

Are you cold?
Heb je het koud?
Heb yuh het kaut?

We can stay out as late as you want.
We kunnen zo laat wegblijven als je wilt.
Vuh KUH-nuhn zoh laht VEG-blai-fuhn ahls yuh vilt.

Please, dinner is on me.
Alsjeblieft, ik trakteer je op het etentje.
Ahs-yuh-BLEEFT, ik trahk-TEYR yuh ohp het EY-tuhn-tyuh.

Shall we split the bill?
Zullen we de rekening splitsen?
ZUH-luhn vuh duh REY-kuh-ning SPLIT-suhn?

We should spend more time together.
We zouden meer tijd samen moeten doorbrengen.
Vuh ZAU-duhn meyr tait SAH-muhn MOO-tuhn DOHR-breng-uhn.

We should walk the town tonight.
We moeten vanavond door de stad lopen.
Vuh MOO-tuhn fahn-AH-vohnt dohr duh staht LOH-puhn.

Did you enjoy everything?
Heb je van alles genoten?
Heb yuh fahn AH-luhs guh-NOH-tuhn?

MONEY AND SHOPPING

May I try this on?
Mag ik dit passen?
Mahg ik dit PAH-suhn?

How much does this cost?
Hoeveel kost dit?
HOO-feyl kohst dit?

Do I sign here or here?
Moet ik hier of hier tekenen?
MOOT ik heer ohf heer TEY-kuh-nun?

Is that your final price?
Is dat je laagste prijs?
Is daht yuh LAHG-stuh prais?

Where do I find toiletries?
Waar vind ik toiletartikelen?
Vahr fint ik twah-LET-ahr-tee-kuh-luhn?

Would you be willing to take five dollars for this item?
Zou je bereid zijn om vijf dollar aan te nemen voor dit artikel?
Zau yuh buh-RAIT sain ohm faif DOH-lahr ahn tuh NEY-muhn fohr dit ahr-TEE-kuhl?

I can't afford it at that price.
Ik kan het me niet veroorloven voor die prijs.
Ik kahn het muh neet ver-OHR-loh-vuhn fohr dee prais.

I can find this cheaper somewhere else.
Ik kan dit ergens anders goedkoper vinden.
Ik kahn dit ER-guhns AHN-duhrs goot-KOH-puhr FIN-duhn.

Is there a way we can haggle on price?
Kunnen we op prijs afdingen?
KUH-nuhn vuh ohp prais AHF-ding-uhn?

How many of these have sold today?

Hoeveel van deze zijn er vandaag verkocht?

HOO-feyl fahn DEY-zuh sain er fahn-DAHG fer-KOHGT?

Can you wrap that up as a gift?

Kun je dat als cadeau inpakken?

Kuhn yuh daht ahls kah-DOH IN-pah-kuhn?

Do you provide personalized letters?

Verstrekt u gepersonaliseerde brieven?

Ver-STREKT oo guh-per-soh-nah-lee-seyr-duh BREE-fuhn?

I would like this to be special delivered to my hotel.

Ik wil graag dat dit speciaal wordt afgeleverd bij mijn hotel.

Ik vil grahg daht dit spey-SYAHL wohrt AHF-guh-ley-fuhrt bai main hoh-TEL.

Can you help me, please?

Kan je me alsjeblieft helpen?

Kahn yuh muh ahs-yuh-BLEEFT HEL-puhn?

We should go shopping at the market.

We moeten gaan winkelen op de markt.

Vuh MOO-tuhn gahn ahs-yuh-BLEEFT VING-kuh-luhn ohp duh mahrkt.

Are you keeping track of the clothes that fit me?

Houdt u bij welke kleding me past?

Haut oo bai VEL-kuh KLEY-ding muh pahst?

Can I have one size up?

Kan ik één maat groter hebben?

Kahn ik eyn maht GROH-tuhr HE-buhn?

How many bathrooms does the apartment have?

Hoeveel badkamers heeft het appartement?

HOO-feyl BAHT-kah-muhrs heyft het ah-pahr-tuh-MENT?

Where's the kitchen?

Waar is de keuken?

Vahr is duh KUH-kuhn?

Does this apartment have a gas or electric stove?

Heeft dit appartement een gas- of elektrisch fornuis?

Heyft dit ah-pahr-tuh-MENT uhn gahs ohf ey-LEK-trees fohr-NUIS?

Is there a spacious backyard?
Is er een ruime achtertuin?
Is er uhn RUI-muh AHG-tuhr-tuin?

How much is the down payment?
Hoeveel bedraagt de borg?
HOO-feyl buh-DRAHGT duh bohrg?

I'm looking for a furnished apartment.
Ik zoek een gemeubileerd appartement.
Ik zook uhn guh-MUH-bee-leyrt ah-pahr-tuh-MENT.

I need a two-bedroom apartment to rent.
Ik heb een appartement met twee slaapkamers nodig om te huren.
Ik heb uhn ah-pahr-tuh-MENT met tvey SLAHP-kah-muhrs NOH-duhg ohm tuh HEW-ruhn.

I'm looking for an apartment with utilities paid.
Ik zoek een appartement met betaalde nutsvoorzieningen.
Ik zook uhn ah-par-tuh-MENT met buh-TAHL-duh NUHTS-fohr-zee-ning-uhn.

The carpet in this apartment needs to be pulled up.
Het tapijt in dit appartement moet worden vervangen.
Het tah-PAIT in dit ah-pahr-tuh-MENT moot VOHR-duhn fer-FAHNG-uhn.

I need you to come down on the price of this apartment.
Je moet de prijs van dit appartement verlagen.
Yuh moot duh prais fahn dit ah-par-tuh-MENT fer-LAH-guhn.

Will I be sharing this place with other people?
Zal ik deze plek met andere mensen moeten delen?
Zahl ik DEY-zuh plek met AHN-duh-ruh MEN-suhn MOO-tuhn DEY-luhn?

How do you work the fireplace?
Hoe werkt de open haard?
Hoo verkt duh OH-puhn hahrt?

Are there any curfew rules attached to this apartment?
Zijn er regels voor avondklok verbonden aan dit appartement?
Sain er REY-guhls fohr AH-fohnt-klohk fer-BOHN-duhn ahn dit ah-pahr-tuh-MENT?

How long is the lease for this place?
Hoe lang is de huurovereenkomst voor deze plek?
Hoo lahng is duh HEWR-oh-fuhr-eyn-kohmst fohr DEY-zuh plek?

Do you gamble?
Gok je?
Gohk yuh?

We should go to a casino.
We moeten naar een casino gaan.
Vuh MOO-tuhn nahr uhn kah-SEE-no gahn.

There is really good horse racing in this area.
Er zijn hele goede paardenraces in dit gebied.
Er sain HEY-luh GOO-duh PAHR-duhn-rey-suhs in dit guh-beet.

Do you have your ID so that we can go gambling?
Heb je je identiteitsbewijs zodat we kunnen gaan gokken?
Heb yuh yuh ee-den-tee-TAITS-buh-vais zoh-DAHT vuh KUH-nuhn gahn GOH-kuhn?

Who did you bet on?
Op wie heb je gewed?
Ohp vee heb yuh guh-WET?

I am calling about the apartment that you placed in the ad.
Ik bel over het appartement dat u in de advertentie heeft gezet.
Ik bel OH-fuhr het ah-pahr-tuh-MENT daht oo in duh aht-fuhr-TENT-see heyft guh-ZET.

How much did you bet?
Hoeveel heb je ingezet?
Hoo-FEYL heb yuh IN-guh-zet?

We should go running with the bulls!
Laten we gaan rennen met de stieren!
LAH-tuhn vuh gahn RE-nuhn met duh STEE-ruhn!

Is Adele coming to sing at this venue tonight?
Komt Adele vanavond zingen in deze zaal?
Kohmt ah-DEL fahn-AH-fohnt ZING-uhn in DEY-zuh zahl?

How much is the item you have in the window?
Hoeveel kost het artikel in de etalage heeft?
HOO-feyl kohst het ahr-TEE-kuhl in duh EH-tah-lah-syuh heyft?

Do you have payment plans?
Heeft u een betalingsregeling?
Heyft oo buh-TAH-lings-rey-guh-ling?

Do these two items come together?
Horen deze twee artikelen bij elkaar?
Hoh-ruhn DEY-zuh tvey ahr-TEE-kuh-luhn bai el-KAHR?

Are these parts cheaply made?
Zijn deze onderdelen goedkoop gemaakt?
Sain DEY-zuh OHN-duhr-dey-luhn goot-KOHP guh-MAHKT?

This is a huge bargain!
Dit is een koopje!
Dit is uhn KOHP-yuh!

I like this. How does three hundred dollars sound?
Ik vind deze mooi. Wat vindt u van driehonderd dollar?
Ik find DEY-zuh mohee. Vaht fint oo vahn DREE-hohn-duhrt DOH-lahr?

Two hundred is all I can offer. That is my final price.
Tweehonderd is alles wat ik kan bieden. Dat is mijn laatste bod.
TVEY-hohn-duhrt is AH-luhs vaht ik kahn BEE-duhn. Daht is main LAHT-stuh boht.

Do you have cheaper versions of this item?
Heeft u goedkopere versies van dit artikel?
Heyft oo goot-KOH-puh-ruh FER-sees fahn dit ahr-TEE-kuhl?

Do you have the same item with a different pattern?
Heeft u hetzelfde artikel met een ander patroon?
Heyft oo het-ZELF-duh ahr-TEE-kuhl met uhn AHN-duhr pah-TROHN?

How much is this worth?
Hoeveel is dit waard?
HOO-feyl is dit vahrt?

Can you pack this up and send it to my address on file?
Kun je dit inpakken en naar mijn geregistreerde adres sturen?
Kuhn yuh dit IN-pah-kuhn en nahr main guh-REY-gee-streyr-duh ah-DRES STOO-ruhn?

Does it fit?
Past het?
Pahst het?

They are too big for me.
Ze zijn te groot voor mij.
Zuh sain tuh groht fohr mai.

Please find me another but in the same size.
Zoek alstublieft een andere voor me, maar in dezelfde maat.
Zook ahs-too-BLEEFT uhn AHN-duh-ruh fohr muh, mahr in duh-ZELF-duh maht.

It fits, but is tight around my waist.
Het past, maar zit strak om mijn middel.
Het pahst, mahr zit strahk ohm main MI-duhl.

Can I have one size down?
Kan ik een maat kleiner krijgen?
Kahn ik uhn maht KLAI-nuhr KRAI-guhn?

Size twenty, American.
Maat twintig, Amerikaanse maat.
Maht TVIN-tig, ah-mey-ree-KAHN-se maht.

Do you sell appliances for the home?
Verkoopt u huishoudelijke apparaten?
Fer-KOHPT oo huis-HAU-duh-luh-kuh ah-pah-RAH-tuhn?

Not now, thank you.
Nu niet, dank je.
Noo neet, dahnk yuh.

I'm looking for something special.
Ik zoek iets speciaals.
Ik zook eets spey-SYAHLS.

I'll call you when I need you.
Ik bel je wanneer ik je nodig heb.
Ik bel yuh VAH-neyr ik yuh NOH-duhg heb.

Do you have this in my size?
Heeft u dit in mijn maat?
Heyft oo dit in main maht?

On which floor can I find cologne?
Op welke verdieping kan ik parfum vinden?
Ohp VEL-kuh fuhr-DEE-ping kahn ik pahr-FUHM FIN-duhn?

Where is the entrance?
Waar is de ingang?
Vahr is duh IN-gahng?

Do I exit from that door?
Kan ik door die deur naar buiten?
Kahn ik dohr dee duhr nahr BUI-tuhn?

Where is the elevator?
Waar is de lift?
Vahr is duh lift?

Do I push or pull to get this door open?
Moet ik duwen of trekken om deze deur open te krijgen?
Moot ik DOO-vuhn ohf TRE-kuhn ohm DEY-zuh duhr OH-puhn tuh KRAI-guhn?

I already have that, thanks.
Ik heb dat al, bedankt.
Ik heb daht ahl, buh-DAHNKT.

Where can I try this on?
Waar kan ik dit passen?
Vahr kahn ik dit PAH-suhn?

This mattress is very soft.
Dit matras is heel zacht.
Dit mah-TRAHS is heyl zahgt.

What is a good place for birthday gifts?
Wat is een goede winkel voor verjaardagsgeschenken?
Vaht is uhn GOO-duh win-kuhl fohr fuhr-YAHR-dahgs-guh-sgeng-kuhn?

I'm just looking, but thank you.
Ik ben alleen aan het kijken, maar bedankt.
Ik ben ah-LEYN ahn het KAI-kuhn, buh-DAHNKT.

Yes, I will call you when I need you, thank you.
Ja, ik roep je wanneer ik je nodig heb, dank je.
Yah, ik roop yuh VAH-neyr ik yuh NOH-duhg heb, dahnk yuh.

Do you accept returns?
Accepteert u retouren?
Ahk-sep-TEYRT oo ruh-TOO-ruhn?

Here is my card and receipt for the return.
Hier zijn mijn kaart en bon voor het retourneren.
Heer sain main kahrt en bohn fohr het rey-toor-NEY-ruhn.

Where are the ladies' clothes?
Waar is de dameskleding?
Vahr is duh DAH-muhs-kley-ding?

What sizes are available for this item?
Welke maten zijn er beschikbaar voor dit artikel?
VEL-kuh MAH-tuhn sain er buh-SGIK-bahr fohr dit ahr-TEE-kuhl?

Is there an ATM machine nearby?
Is er een geldautomaat in de buurt?
Is er uhn GELT-au-toh-maht in duh buhrt?

What forms of payment do you accept?
Welke betalingsmethoden accepteert u?
VEL-kuh buh-TAH-lings-mey-toh-duhn ahk-sep-TEYRT oo?

That doesn't interest me.
Dat interesseert me niet.
Daht in-tuh-ruh-SEYRT muh neet.

I don't like it, but thank you.
Ik vind het niet mooi, maar bedankt.
Ik fint het neet mohee, mahr buh-DAHNKT.

Do you take American dollars?
Accepteert u Amerikaanse dollars?
Ahk-sep-TEYRT oo ah-mey-ree-KAHN-suh DOH-lahrs?

Can you make change for me?
Kunt u me kleingeld geven?
Kuhnt oo muh KLAIN-gelt GEY-fuhn?

What is the closest place to get change for my money?
Wat is de dichtstbijzijnde plaats om kleingeld te krijgen?
Vaht is duh DIGTST-bai-zain-duh plahts ohm KLAIN-gelt tuh KRAI-guhn?

Are travelers checks able to be changed here?
Kunnen reischeques hier worden ingewisseld?
KUH-nuhn RAIS-syeks heer VOHR-duhn IN-guh-vi-suhlt?

What is the current exchange rate?
Wat is de huidige wisselkoers?
Vaht is duh HUI-duh-guh VI-suhl-koors?

What is the closest place to exchange money?
Wat is de dichtstbijzijnde plaats om geld te wisselen?
Vaht is duh DIGTST-bai-sain-duh plahts ohm gelt tuh VI-suh-luhn?

Do you need to borrow money? How much?
Moet je geld lenen? Hoe veel?
Moot yuh gelt LEY-nuhn? Hoo feyl?

Can this bank exchange my money?
Kan deze bank mijn geld wisselen?
Kahn DEY-zuh bahnk main gelt VI-suh-luhn?

What is the exchange rate for the American dollar?
Wat is de wisselkoers van de Amerikaanse dollar?
Vaht is duh VI-suhl-koors fahn duh ah-mey-ree-KAHN-suh DOH-lahr?

Will you please exchange me fifty dollars?
Kunt u alstublieft vijftig dollar omwisselen?
Kuhnt oo ahs-too-BLEEFT FAIF-tuhg DOH-lahr OHM-vi-suh-luhn?

I would like a receipt with that.
Daar zou ik graag een ontvangstbewijs voor willen hebben.
Dahr zau ik grahg uhn ohnt-FAHNGST-buh-vais fohr VI-luhn HE-buhn.

Your commission rate is too high.
Uw commissie is te hoog.
Ew koh-MI-see is tuh hohg.

Does this bank have a lower commission rate?
Heeft deze bank een lagere commissie?
Heyft DEY-zuh bahnk uhn LAH-guh-ruh koh-MI-see?

Do you take cash?
Neem je contant geld aan?
Neym yuh kohn-TAHNT gelt ahn?

Where can I exchange dollars?
Waar kan ik dollars wisselen?
Vahr kahn ik DOH-lahrs VI-suh-luhn?

I want to exchange dollars for euros.
Ik wil dollars inwisselen voor euro's.
Ik vil DOH-lahrs IN-vi-suh-luhn fohr UH-rohs.

Do you take credit cards?
Accepteert u creditcards?
Ak-sep-TEYRT oo KRE-dit-kahrts?

Here is my credit card.
Hier is mijn creditcard.
Heer is main KRE-dit-kahrt.

One moment, let me check the receipt.
Laat me even de bon controleren.
Laht muh EY-fuhn duh bohn kohn-troh-LEY-ruhn.

Do I need to pay tax?
Moet ik btw betalen?
Moot ik BEY-tey-vey buh-TAH-luhn?

How much is this item with tax?
Hoeveel kost dit artikel met btw?
HOO-feyl kohst dit ar-TEE-kuhl met BEY-tey-wet?

Where is the cashier?
Waar is de kassier?
Vahr is duh kah-SYEER?

Excuse me, I'm looking for a dress.
Pardon, ik zoek een jurk.
Pahr-DON, ik zook uhn yuhrk.

That's a lot for that dress.
Dat is duur voor die jurk.
Daht is duhr fohr dee yuhrk.

Sorry, but I don't want it.
Sorry, maar ik wil het niet.
SOH-ree, mahr ik vil het neet.

Okay I will take it.
Oké, ik neem het.
Oh-KEY, ik neym het.

I'm not interested if you are going to sell it at that price.
Ik hoef het niet als u het voor die prijs verkoopt.
Ik hoof het neet ahls oo het fohr dee prais fer-KOHPT.

You are cheating me at the current price.
U bedriegt me met de huidige prijs.
Oo buh-DREEGT muh met duh HUI-duh-guh prais.

No thanks. I'll only take it if you lower the price by half.
Nee, dank u wel. Ik neem het alleen als u de prijs met de helft verlaagt.
Ney, dahnk oo vel. Ik neym het ah-LEYN ahls oo duh prais met duh helft fuhr-LAHGT.

That is a good price, I'll take it.
Dat is een goede prijs, ik neem het.
Daht is uhn GOO-duh prais, ik neym het.

Do you sell souvenirs for tourists?
Verkoopt u souvenirs voor toeristen?
Fuhr-KOHPT oo soo-vuh-NEERS fohr too-RIS-tuhn?

Can I have a bag for that?
Mag ik daar een tasje voor hebben?
Mahg ik dahr uhn TAHS-yuh fohr HE-buhn?

Is this the best bookstore in the city?
Is dit de beste boekwinkel van de stad?
Is dit duh BES-tuh BOO-kuhn-ving-kuhl fahn duh staht?

I would like to go to a game shop to buy comic books.
Ik zou graag naar een gamewinkel gaan om stripboeken te kopen.
Ik zau grahg nahr uhn geym-ving-kuhl gahn ohm STRIP-boo-kuhn tuh KOH-puhn.

Are you able to ship my products overseas?
Kunt u mijn producten naar het buitenland verzenden?
Kuhnt oo main proh-DUHK-tuhn nahr het BUI-tuhn-lahnt fuhr-ZEN-duhn?

CHILDREN AND PETS

Which classroom does my child attend?
Naar welk klaslokaal gaat mijn kind?
Nahr velk KLAHS-loh-kahl gaht main kint?

Is the report due before the weekend?
Moet het verslag voor het weekend worden ingediend?
Moot het fer-SLAHG fohr het WEE-kent WOHR-duhn IN-guh-deent?

I'm waiting for my mom to pick me up.
Ik wacht tot mijn moeder me ophaalt.
Ik wagt toht main MOO-duhr muh OHP-hahlt.

What time does the school bus run?
Hoe laat komt de schoolbus?
Hoo laht kohmt duh SGOHL-buhs?

I need to see the principal.
Ik moet de directeur zien.
Ik moot duh di-rek-TUHR zeen.

I would like to report bullying.
Ik wil een melding maken van pesten.
Ik vil uhn MEL-ding MAH-kuhn fahn PES-tuhn.

What are the leash laws in this area?
Moet mijn hond in dit gebied worden aangelijnd?
Moot main hohnt in dit guh-BEET WOHR-duhn AHN-guh-laint?

Please keep your dog away from mine.
Houd alstublieft uw hond uit de buurt van de mijne.
Haut ahs-too-BLEEFT ew hohnt uit duh boort fahn duh MAI-nuh.

My dog doesn't bite.
Mijn hond bijt niet.
Main hohnt bait neet.

I am allergic to cat hair.
Ik ben allergisch voor kattenhaar.
Ik ben ah-LER-gees fohr KAH-tuhn-hahr.

Don't leave the door open or the cat will run out!
Laat de deur niet openstaan, anders loopt de kat weg!
Laht duh duhr neet OH-puhn-stahn, AHN-duhrs lohpt duh kaht veg!

Have you fed the dogs yet?
Heb je de honden al gevoerd?
Heb yuh duh HOHN-duhn ahl guh-FOORT?

We need to take the dog to the veterinarian.
We moeten de hond naar de dierenarts brengen.
Vuh MOO-tuhn duh hohnt nahr duh DEE-ruhn-ahrts BRENG-uhn.

Are there any open roster spots on the team?
Zijn er plekken open voor vaste teamspelers?
Sain er PLE-kuhn OH-puhn fohr FAHS-tuh teem-SPEY-luhrs?

My dog is depressed.
Mijn hond is depressief.
Main hohnt is dey-pruh-SEEF.

Don't feed the dog table scraps.
Geef de hond geen etensresten.
Geyf duh hohnt geyn EY-tuhns-res-tuhn.

Don't let the cat climb up on the furniture.
Laat de kat niet op het meubilair klimmen.
Laht duh kaht neet ohp het muh-bee-LAIR KLI-muhn.

The dog is not allowed to sleep in the bed with you.
De hond mag niet bij jou in bed slapen.
Duh hohnt mahg neet bai yau in bet SLAH-puhn.

There is dog poop on the floor. Clean it up.
Er ligt hondenpoep op de grond. Maak het schoon.
Er ligt HOHN-duhn-poop ohp duh grohnt. Mahk het sgohn.

When was the last time you took the dog for a walk?
Wanneer heb je voor het laatst de hond uitgelaten?
Vah-NEYR heb yuh fohr het laatst duh hohnt uit-guh-LAH-tuhn?

Are you an international student? How long are you attending?
Ben jij een internationale student? Voor hoe lang ben je hier?
Ben yai uhn IN-tuhr-nah-syo-nah-luh stoo-DENT? Fohr hoo lahng ben yuh heer?

Are you a French student?
Ben je een Franse student?
Ben yuh uhn FRAHN-suh stoo-DENT?

I am an American student that is here for the semester.
Ik ben een Amerikaanse student die hier is voor dit semester.
Ik ben uhn a-mey-ree-KAHN-suh stoo-DENT dee heer is fohr dit suh-MES-tuhr.

Please memorize this information.
Onthoud alsjeblieft deze informatie.
Ont-HAUT ahs-yuh-BLEEFT DEY-zuh in-fohr-MAHT-see.

This is my roommate Max.
Dit is mijn kamergenoot Max.
Dit is main KAH-muhr-guh-noht max.

Are these questions likely to appear on the exams?
Is het waarschijnlijk dat deze vragen op de examens verschijnen?
Is het vahr-SGAIN-luhk daht DEY-zuh VRAH-guhn op duh ek-SAH-muhns fuhr-SGAI-nuhn?

Teacher, say that once more, please.
Leraar, zeg dat nog eens, alstublieft.
LEY-rahr, zeg daht nohg eyns, ahs-too-BLEEFT.

I didn't do well on the quiz.
Mijn toets is niet goed gegaan.
Main toots is neet goot guh-GAHN.

Go play outside, but stay where I can see you.
Ga maar buiten spelen, maar zo dat ik je kan zien.
Gah mahr BUI-tuhn SPEY-luhn, mahr zo daht ik je kahn zeen.

How is your daughter?
Hoe gaat het met je dochter?
Hoo gaht het met yuh DOHG-tuhr?

I'm going to walk the dogs.
Ik ga de honden uitlaten.
Ik gah duh HOHN-duhn UIT-lah-tuhn.

She's not very happy here.
Ze is hier niet erg gelukkig.
Zuh is heer neet erg guh-LUH-kig.

I passed the quiz with high marks!
Ik ben met een hoog cijfer geslaagd voor het examen!
Ik ben met uhn HOHG SAI-fuhr guh-slahgt fohr het ex-AH-muhn.

What program are you enrolled in?
Bij welk programma ben je ingeschreven?
Bai velk proh-GRAH-mah ben yuh IN-guh-sgrey-vuhn?

I really like my English teacher.
Ik vind mijn leraar Engels heel leuk.
Ik fint main LEY-rahr ENG-uhls heyl luhk.

I have too much homework to do.
Ik heb te veel huiswerk.
Ik heb tuh-FEYL HUIS-verk.

Tomorrow, I have to take my dog to the vet.
Morgen moet ik mijn hond naar de dierenarts brengen.
MOHR-guhn moot ik main hohnt nahr duh DEE-ruhn-ahrts BRENG-uhn.

When do we get to go to lunch?
Wanneer gaan we lunchen?
Vah-NEYR gahn vuh LUHN-syuhn?

My dog swallowed something he shouldn't have.
Mijn hond heeft iets ingeslikt dat hij niet had moeten eten.
Main hohnt heyft eets IN-guh-slikt daht hai neet haht MOO-tuhn EY-tuhn.

We need more toys for our dog to play with.
We hebben meer speelgoed nodig waar onze hond mee kan spelen.
Vuh HE-buhn meyr SPEYL-goot NOH-duhg vahr ON-zuh hohnt mey kahn SPEY-luhn.

Can you please change the litter box?
Kun je de kattenbak alsjeblieft verschonen?
Kuhn yuh duh KAH-tuhn-bahk ahs-yuh-BLEEFT fuhr-SGOH-nuhn?

Get a lint brush and roll it to get the hair off your clothes.
Pak een pluisborstel en rol deze om het haar van je kleding te halen.
Pahk uhn PLUIS-bohrs-tuhl en rohl DEY-zuh ohm het hahr fahn yuh KLEY-ding tuh HAH-luhn.

Can you help me study?
Kunt u mij helpen met studeren?
Kuhnt oo mai HEL-puhn met stoo-DEY-ruhn?

I have to go study in my room.
Ik moet in mijn kamer gaan studeren.
Ik moot in main KAH-muhr gahn stoo-DEY-ruhn.

We went to the campus party, and it was a lot of fun.
We gingen naar het campusfeest en het was erg leuk.
Vuh GING-uhn nahr het KAHM-pus-feyst en het vahs erg luhk.

Can you use that word in a sentence?
Kun je dat woord in een zin gebruiken?
Kuhn yuh daht vohrt in uhn zin guh-BRUI-kuhn?

How do you spell that word?
Hoe spel je dat woord?
Hoo spel yuh daht vohrt?

Go play with your brother.
Ga met je broer spelen.
Gah met yuh broor SPEY-luhn.

Come inside! It is dinnertime.
Kom binnen! Het is etenstijd.
Kohm BI-nuhn! Het is EY-tuhns-tait.

Tell me about your day.
Vertel mij over jouw dag.
Fuhr-TEL mai OH-fuhr yau dahg.

Is there anywhere you want to go?
Waar wil je heen?
Vahr vil yuh heyn?

How are you feeling?
Hoe voel je je?
Hoo fool yuh yuh?

117

What do you want me to make for dinner tonight?
Wat wil je dat ik vanavond voor het avondeten maak?
Vaht vil yuh daht ik fahn-AH-fohnt fohr het AH-fohnt-ey-tuhn mahk?

It's time for you to take a bath.
Het wordt tijd dat je een bad neemt.
Het vohrt tait daht yuh uhn baht neymt.

Brush your teeth and wash behind your ears.
Poets je tanden en was je achter je oren.
Poots yuh TAHN-duhn en vahs yuh AHG-tuhr yuh OH-ruhn.

You're not wearing that to bed.
Dat doe je niet aan naar bed.
Daht doo yuh neet ahn nahr bet.

I don't like the way you're dressed. Put something else on.
Ik hou niet van de manier waarop je gekleed bent. Doe iets anders aan.
Ik hau neet fahn duh mah-NEER VAHR-ohp yuh guh-KLEYT bent. Doo eets AHN-duhrs ahn.

Did you make any friends today?
Heb je vandaag vrienden gemaakt?
Heb yuh fahn-DAHG FREEN-duhn guh-MAHKT?

Let me see your homework.
Laat me je huiswerk zien.
Laht muh yuh HUIS-verk zeen.

Do I need to call your school?
Moet ik je school bellen?
Moot ik yuh sgohl BE-luhn?

The dog can't go outside right now.
De hond kan niet naar buiten op dit moment.
Duh hohnt kahn neet nahr BUI-tuhn ohp dit moh-MENT.

Is the new quiz going to be available next week?
Is het nieuwe examen volgende week beschikbaar?
Is het NEE-wuh ex-AH-muhn FOHL-guhn-duh veyk buh-SGIK-bahr?

Are we allowed to use calculators with the test?
Mogen we rekenmachines gebruiken bij het proefwerk?
MOH-guhn vuh REY-kuhn-mah-syee-nuhs guh-BRUI-kuhn bai het proof-VERK?

I would like to lead today's lesson.
Ik zou graag de les van vandaag willen leiden.
Ik zau grahg duh les fahn fahn-DAHG WI-luhn LAI-duhn.

I have a dorm curfew so I need to go back.
Ik heb een avondklok, dus ik moet terug.
Ik heb uhn AH-fohnt-klohk, duhs ik moot tuh-ruhg.

Do I have to use pencil or ink?
Moet ik een potlood of een pen gebruiken?
Moot ik uhn POHT-loht ohf pen guh-BRUI-khn?

Are cell phones allowed in class?
Zijn mobiele telefoons toegestaan in de klas?
Sain moh-BEE-luh tey-luh-FOHNS TOO-guh-stahn in duh klahs?

Where can I find the nearest dog park?
Waar vind ik het dichtstbijzijnde hondenpark?
Vahr vint ik het DIGTST-bai-sain-duh HOHN-duhn-pahrk?

Are dogs allowed to be off their leash here?
Mogen honden hier loslopen?
MOH-guhn HOHN-duhn heer LOHS-loh-puhn?

Are children allowed here?
Zijn kinderen hier toegestaan?
Sain KIN-duh-run heer TOO-guh-stahn?

I would like to set up a play date with our children.
Ik zou graag een play date met onze kinderen willen afspreken.
Ik zau grahg uhn pley deyt met ON-zuh KIN-duh-run WI-lun AF-sprey-kun.

I would like to invite you to my child's birthday party.
Ik nodig je graag uit voor het verjaardagsfeestje van mijn kind.
Ik NOH-duhg yuh grahg uit fohr het fuhr-YAHR-dahgs-feyst-yuh fahn main kind.

Did you miss your dorm curfew last night?
Heb je gisteravond je avondklok gemist?
Heb yuh gis-tuhr-AH-fohnt yuh AH-fohnt-klohk guh-MIST?

TRAVELER'S GUIDE

Over there is the library.
Daar is de bibliotheek.
Dahr is duh bee-blee-oh-TEYK.

Just over there.
Daarzo.
DAHR-zoh.

Yes, this way.
Ja, deze kant op.
Yah, DEY-zuh kahnt ohp.

I haven't done anything wrong.
Ik heb niets verkeerds gedaan.
Ik heb neets fuhr-KEYRTS guh-DAHN.

It was a misunderstanding.
Het was een misverstand.
Het vahs uhn MIS-fuhr-stahnt.

I am an American citizen.
Ik ben Amerikaans staatsburger.
Ik ben a-mey-ree-KAHNS STAHTS-buhr-guhr.

We are tourists on vacation.
Wij zijn toeristen op vakantie.
Vai sain too-RIS-tuhn ohp vah-KAHN-see.

I am looking for an apartment.
Ik zoek een appartement.
Ik zook uhn ah-par-tuh-MENT.

This is a short-term stay.
Het is een kort verblijf.
Dit is uhn ah-PAHR-tuh-ment fohr kohrt fuhr-BLAIF.

I am looking for a place to rent.
Ik zoek een plek om te huren.
Ik zook uhn plek ohm tuh HEW-ruhn.

Where can we grab a quick bite to eat?
Waar kunnen we een snelle hap eten?
Vahr KUH-nuhn vuh uhn SNE-luh hahp EY-tuhn?

We need the cheapest place you can find.
We hebben de goedkoopste plek nodig die je kunt vinden.
Vuh HE-buhn duh goot-KOHP-stuh plek NOH-duhg dee yuh kuhnt FIN-duhn.

Do you have a map of the city?
Heeft u een plattegrond van de stad?
Heyft oo uhn PLAH-tuh-grohnt fahn duh staht?

What places do tourists usually visit when they come here?
Welke plaatsen bezoeken toeristen meestal als ze hier komen?
VEL-kuh PLAHT-suhn buh-ZOO-kuhn too-RIS-tuhn MEY-stahl ahls zuh heer KOH-muhn?

Can you take our picture, please?
Wil je alsjeblieft een foto van ons maken?
Vil yuh ahs-yuh-BLEEFT uhn FOH-toh fahn ohns MAH-kuhn?

Do you take foreign credit cards?
Accepteert u buitenlandse creditcards?
Ahk-sep-TEYRT oo BUI-tuhn-lahnt-suh KRE-dit-kahrts?

I would like to hire a bicycle to take us around the city.
Ik wil graag een fiets huren om de stad te verkennen.
Ik zau grahg uhn feets HOO-ruhn ohm duh staht tuh ver-ken-nuhn.

Do you mind if I take pictures here?
Vind je het erg als ik hier foto's maak?
Fint yuh het erg ahls ik heer FOH-tohs mahk?

ANSWERS

Yes, to some extent.
Ja, tot op zekere hoogte.
Yah, toht ohp ZEY-kuh-ruh HOHG-tuh.

I'm not sure.
Ik weet het niet zeker
Ik veyt het neet ZEY-kuhr.

Yes, go ahead.
Ja, ga je gang.
Yah, gah yuh gahng.

Yes, just like you.
Ja, net zoals jij.
Yah, net ZOH-ahls yai.

No, no problem at all.
Nee, geen problem.
Ney, geyn proh-BLEYM.

This is a little more expensive than the other item.
Dit is iets duurder dan het andere artikel.
Dit is eets DUHR-duhr dahn het AHN-duh-ruh ahr-TEE-kuhl.

My city is small but nice.
Mijn stad is klein maar fijn.
Main staht is klain mahr fain.

This city is quite big.
Deze stad is vrij groot.
DEY-zuh staht is frai groht.

I'm from America.
Ik kom uit Amerika.
Ik kohm uit ah-MEY-ree-kah.

We'll wait for you.
We zullen op je wachten.
Vuh ZUH-luhn ohp yuh VAHG-tuhn.

I love going for walks.
Ik ga graag wandelen.
Ik gah grahg VAHN-duh-luhn.

I'm a woman.
Ik ben een vrouw.
Ik ben uhn frau.

Good, I'm going to see it.
Goed, ik ga het bekijken.
Goot, ik gah het buh-KAI-kuhn.

So do I.
Ik ook.
Ik ohk.

I'll think about it and call you tomorrow with an answer.
Ik denk erover na en bel je morgen met een antwoord.
Ik denk er-OH-fuhr nah en bel yuh MOHR-guhn met uhn AHNT-vohrt.

I have two children.
Ik heb twee kinderen.
Ik heb tvey KIN-duh-ruhn.

Does this place have a patio?
Heeft deze plek een patio?
Heyft DEY-zuh plek uhn PAH-tee-oh?

No, the bathroom is vacant.
Nee, de badkamer is vrij.
Ney, duh BAHT-kah-muhr is frai.

I'm not old enough.
Ik ben niet oud genoeg.
Ik ben neet aut guh-NOOG.

No, it is very easy.
Nee het is heel makkelijk.
Ney, het is heyl MAH-kuh-luhk.

Understood.
Begrepen.
Buh-GREY-puhn.

Only if you go first.
Alleen als jij eerst gaat.
Ah-LEYN ahls yai eyrst gaht.

Yes, that is correct.
Ja, dat is juist.
Yah, daht is yuist.

That was the wrong answer.
Dat was het verkeerde antwoord.
Daht vahs het fuhr-KEYR-duh AHNT-vohrt.

We haven't decided yet.
We hebben nog niet besloten.
Vuh HE-buhn nohg neet buh-SLOH-tuhn.

We can try.
We kunnen het proberen.
Vuh KUH-nuhn het proh-BEY-ruhn.

I like to read books.
Ik lees graag boeken.
Ik leys grahg BOO-kuhn.

We can go there together.
We kunnen er samen heen gaan.
Vuh KUH-nuhn er SAH-muhn heyn gahn.

Yes, I see.
Ja, ik begrijp het.
Yah, ik buh-GRAIP het.

That looks interesting.
Dat ziet er interessant uit.
Daht zeet er in-tuh-ruh-SAHNT uit.

Me neither.
Ik ook niet.
Ik ohk neet.

It was fun.
Het was leuk.
Het vahs luhk.

Me too.
Ik ook.
Ik ohk.

Stay there.
Blijf hier.
Blaif heer.

We were worried about you.
We waren bezorgd om je.
Vuh VAH-ruhn buh-ZOHRGT ohm yuh.

No, not really.
Nee, niet echt.
Ney, neet egt.

Unbelievable.
Ongelofelijk.
Ohn-guh-LOH-fuh-luk.

No, I didn't make it in time.
Nee, ik heb het niet op tijd gered.
Ney, ik heb het neet op tait guh-RET.

No, you cannot.
Nee, dat mag niet.
Ney, daht mahg neet.

Here you go.
Alsjeblieft.
Ahs-yuh-BLEEFT.

It was good.
Het was goed.
Het vahs goot.

Ask my wife.
Vraag het aan mijn vrouw.
Frahg het ahn main frau.

That's up to him.
Dat is zijn beslissing.
Daht is sain buh-SLI-sing.

That is not allowed.
Dat is niet toegestaan.
Daht is neet TOO-guh-stahn.

You can stay at my place.
Je kunt bij mij blijven.
Yuh kuhnt bai mai BLAI-fuhn.

Only if you want to.
Alleen als jij het wilt.
A-LEYN ahls yai het vilt.

It depends on my schedule.
Het hangt af van mijn rooster.
Het hahngt ahf fahn main ROH-stuhr.

I don't think that's possible.
Ik denk niet dat dat mogelijk is.
Ik denk neet daht daht MOH-guh-luk is.

You're not bothering me.
Ik vind je niet vervelend.
ik fint yuh neet fuhr-fey-luhnd.

The salesman will know.
Deze verkoper zal het weten.
DEY-zuh fer-KOH-puhr zahl het VEY-tuhn.

I have to work.
Ik moet werken.
Ik moot VER-kuhn.

I'm late.
Ik ben laat.
Ik ben laht.

To pray.
Om te bidden.
Ohm tuh BI-duhn.

I'll do my best.
Ik doe mijn best.
Ik doo main best.

DIRECTIONS

Over here.
Hierzo.
HEER-zoh.

Go straight ahead.
Ga rechtdoor.
Gah REGT-dohr.

Follow the straight line.
Volg de rechte lijn.
Fohlg duh REG-tuh lain.

Go halfway around the circle.
Ga halverwege de cirkel.
Gah HAHL-fuhr-vey-guh duh SIR-kuhl.

It is to the left.
Het is aan de linkerkant.
Het is ahn duh LING-kuhr-kahnt.

Where is the party going to be?
Waar zal het feest zijn?
Vahr zahl het feyst sain?

Where is the library situated?
Waar is de bibliotheek?
Vahr is duh bee-blee-oh-TEYK?

It is to the north.
Het is naar het noorden.
Het is nahr het NOHR-duhn.

You can find it down the street.
Je kunt het verderop in de straat vinden.
Yuh kuhnt het fer-duhr-OP in duh straht FIN-duhn.

Go into the city to get there.
Ga de stad in om er te komen.
Gah duh staht in ohm er tuh KOH-muhn.

Where are you now?
Waar ben je nu?
Vahr ben yuh noo?

There is a fire hydrant right in front of me.
Er staat een brandkraan recht voor me.
Er staht uhn BRAHNT-krahn regt fohr muh.

Do you know a shortcut?
Ken je een binnendoorweg?
Ken yuh uhn bi-nuhn-DOHR-veg?

Where is the freeway?
Waar is de snelweg?
Vahr is duh SNEL-veg?

Do I need exact change for the toll?
Moet ik gepast betalen voor de tol?
Moot ik guh-pahst buh-TAH-len fohr duh tohl?

At the traffic light, turn right.
Sla rechtsaf bij het stoplicht.
Slah REGTS-ahf bai het STOHP-ligt.

When you get to the intersection, turn left.
Sla linksaf bij het kruispunt.
Slah LINKS-ahf bai het KRUIS-puhnt.

Stay in your lane until it splits off to the right.
Blijf op uw rijstrook totdat deze zich naar rechts splitst.
Blaif ohp ew RAI-strohk TOHT-daht DEY-zuh zig nahr regts splitst.

Don't go onto the ramp.
Ga niet de oprit op.
Gah neet duh OHP-rit ohp.

You are going in the wrong direction.
Je gaat de verkeerde kant op.
Yuh gaht duh fuhr-KEYR-duh kahnt ohp.

Can you guide me to this location?

Kunt u mij naar deze locatie wijzen?

Kuhnt oo mai nahr DEY-zuh loh-KAHT-see VAI-zuhn?

Stop at the crossroads.

Stop bij het kruispunt.

Stohp bai het KRUIS-puhnt.

You missed our turn. Please turn around.

Je hebt onze afslag gemist. Draai alsjeblieft om.

Yuh hebt OHN-zuh AHF-slahg guh-MIST. Drie ahs-yuh-BLEEFT ohm.

It is illegal to turn here.

Het is illegaal om hier af te slaan.

Het is ee-luh-GAHL ohm heer ahf tuh slahn.

We're lost, could you help us?

We zijn verdwaald, kunt u ons helpen?

Vuh sain fuhr-DVAHLT, kuhnt oo ohns HEL-puhn?

APOLOGIES

Dad, I'm sorry.
Pap, het spijt me.
Pahp, het spait muh.

I apologize for being late.
Mijn excuses dat ik te laat ben.
Main eks-KU-suhs daht ik tuh laht ben.

Excuse me for not bringing money.
Neem me niet kwalijk dat ik geen geld heb meegebracht.
Neym muh neet KWAH-luhk daht ik geyn gelt heb MEY-guh-brahgt.

That was my fault.
Dat was mijn schuld.
Daht vahs main sguhlt.

It won't happen again, I'm sorry.
Sorry, het zal niet weer gebeuren.
SOH-ree, het zahl neet vehr guh-BUH-ruhn.

I won't break another promise.
Ik zal niet nog een belofte breken.
Ik zahl neet nohg uhn buh-LOHF-tuh BREY-kuhn.

You have my word that I'll be careful.
Je hebt mijn woord dat ik voorzichtig zal zijn.
Yuh hebt main vohrt daht ik fohr-ZIG-tuhg zahl sain.

I'm sorry, I wasn't paying attention.
Het spijt me, ik lette niet op.
Het spait muh, ik LE-tuh neet ohp.

I regret that. I'm so sorry.
Ik heb daar spijt van. Het spijt me zeer.
Ik heb dahr spait fahn. Het spait muh zeyr.

I'm sorry, but today I can't.
Sorry, maar vandaag kan ik niet.
SOH-ree mahr fahn-DAHG kahn ik neet.

It's not your fault, I'm sorry.
Het is niet jouw schuld, sorry.
Het is neet yau sguhlt, SOH-ree.

Please, give me another chance.
Geef me alsjeblieft nog een kans.
Geyf muh ahs-syuh-BLEEFT nohg uhn kahns.

Will you ever forgive me?
Zal je me ooit vergeven?
Zahl yuh muh ooeet fuhr-GEY-fuhn?

I hope in time we can still be friends.
Ik hoop dat we na verloop van tijd nog vrienden kunnen zijn.
Ik hohp dat vuh nah fuhr-LOHP fahn tait nohg FREEN-duhn KUH-nuhn sain.

I screwed up, and I'm sorry.
Ik heb het verknald en het spijt me.
Ik heb het fuhr-KNAHLT en het spait muh.

SMALL TALK

No.
Nee.
Ney.

Yes.
Ja.
Yah.

Okay.
Oké.
Oh-KEY.

Please.
Alsjeblieft.
Ahs-yuh-BLEEFT.

Do you fly out of the country often?
Vlieg je vaak het land uit?
Fleeg yuh fahk het lahnt uit?

Thank you.
Dankjewel.
Dahnk-yuh-VEL.

That's okay.
Dat is oké.
Daht is oh-KEY.

I went shopping.
Ik heb gewinkeld.
Ik heb guh-WING-kuhlt.

There.
Daar.
Dahr.

Very well.
Heel goed.
Heyl goot.

What?
Wat?
Vaht?

I think you'll like it.
Ik denk dat je het leuk zal vinden.
Ik denk daht yuh het luhk zahl FIN-duhn.

When?
Wanneer?
Vah-NEYR?

I didn't sleep well.
Ik heb slecht geslapen.
Ik heb slegt guh-SLAH-puhn.

Until what time?
Tot hoe laat?
Toht hoo laht?

We are waiting in line.
We wachten in de rij.
Vuh VAHG-tuhn in duh rai.

We're only waiting for a little bit longer.
We wachten maar een beetje langer.
Vuh VAHG-tuhn mahr uhn BEYT-yuh LAHNG-uhr.

How?
Hoe?
Hoo?

Where?
Waar?
Vahr?

I'm glad.
Ik ben blij.
Ik ben blai.

You are very tall.
Je bent heel lang.
Yuh bent heyl lahng.

I like to speak your language.
Ik vind het leuk om je taal te spreken.
Ik fint het luhk ohm yuh tahl tuh SPREY-kuhn.

You are very kind.
Je bent erg vriendelijk.
Yuh bent erg FREEN-duh-luhk.

Happy birthday!
Gefeliciteerd!
Guh-fey-lee-see-TEYRT!

I would like to thank you very much.
Ik wil je heel erg bedanken.
Ik vil yuh heyl erg buh-DAHNG-kuhn.

Here is a gift that I bought for you.
Hier is een cadeau dat ik voor je heb gekocht.
Heer is uhn kah-DOH daht ik fohr yuh heb guh-KOHGT.

Yes. Thank you for all of your help.
Ja. Bedankt voor al je hulp.
Yah. Buh-DAHNKT fohr ahl yuh huhlp.

What did you get?
Wat heb je gekregen?
Vaht heb yuh guh-KREY-guhn?

Have a good trip!
Goede reis!
GOO-duh rais!

This place is very special to me.
Deze plek is heel speciaal voor mij.
DEY-zuh plek is heyl spey-SYAHL fohr mai.

My foot is asleep.
Mijn voet slaapt.
Main foot slahpt.

May I open this now or later?
Mag ik dit nu openen of straks pas?
Mahg ik dit noo OH-puh-nuhn ohf strahks pahs?

Why do you think that is?
Waarom denk je dat dat zo is?
Vah-ROHM denk yuh daht daht zoh is?

Which do you like better, chocolate or caramel?
Wat vind je lekkerder, chocolade of karamel?
Vaht fint yuh LE-kuhr-duhr, syoh-koh-LAH-duh ohf kah-rah-MEL?

Be safe on your journey.
Wees veilig tijdens je reis.
Veys FAI-luhg TAI-duhns yuh rais.

I want to do this for a little longer.
Ik wil dit iets langer doen.
Ik vil dit eets LAHNG-uhr doon.

This is a picture that I took at the hotel.
Dit is een foto die ik in het hotel heb gemaakt.
Dit is uhn FOH-toh dee ik in het hoh-TEL heb guh-MAHKT.

Allow me.
Sta me toe.
Stah muh too.

I was surprised.
Ik was verrast.
Ik vahs fuh-RAHST.

I like that.
Ik vind dat leuk.
Ik fint daht luhk.

Are you in high spirits today?
Ben je vandaag opgewekt?
Ben yuh fahn-DAHG OHP-guh-wekt?

Oh, here comes my wife.
Oh, hier komt mijn vrouw.
Oh, heer kohmt main frau.

Can I see the photograph?
Mag ik de foto zien?
Mahg ik duh FOH-toh zeen?

Feel free to ask me anything.
Vraag me gerust iets.
Frahg muh guh-RUHST eets.

That was magnificent!
Dat was schitterend!
Daht vahs SGI-tuh-ruhnd.

See you some other time.
Ik zie je een andere keer.
Ik zee yuh uhn AHN-duh-ruh keyr.

No more, please.
Niet meer, alstublieft.
Neet meyr, ahs-too-BLEEFT.

Please don't use that.
Gebruik dat alsjeblieft niet.
Guh-BRUIK daht ahs-yuh-BLEEFT neet.

That is very pretty.
Dat is erg mooi.
Daht is erg mohee.

Would you say that again?
Wil je dat nog eens zeggen?
Vil yuh daht nohg eyns ZE-guhn?

Speak slowly.
Spreek langzaam.
Spreyk LAHNG-zahm.

I'm home.
Ik ben thuis.
Ik ben tuis.

Is this your home?
Is dit je huis?
Is dit yuh huis?

I know a lot about the area.
Ik weet veel van het gebied.
Ik veyt feyl fahn het guh-BEET.

Welcome back. How was your day?
Welkom terug. Hoe was je dag?
VEL-kohm tuh-RUHG. Hoo vahs yuh dahg?

I read every day.
Ik lees elke dag.
Ik leys EL-kuh dahg.

My favorite type of book is novels by Stephen King.
Mijn favoriete boeksoort zijn romans van Stephen King.
Main FAH-foh-ree-tuh BOOK-sohrt sain roh-MAHNS fahn Stephen King.

You surprised me!
Je verraste me!
Yuh vuh-RAHS-tuh muh!

I am short on time so I have to go.
Ik heb weinig tijd, dus ik moet gaan.
Ik heb VAI-nuhg tait, duhs ik moot gahn.

Thank you for having this conversation.
Bedankt voor dit gesprek.
Buh-DAHNKT fohr dit guh-SPREK.

Oh, when is it?
Oh, wanneer is het?
Oh, vah-NEYR is het?

This is my brother, Jeremy.
Dit is mijn broer, Jeremy.
Dit is main broor, YE-re-mee.

That is my favorite bookstore.
Dat is mijn favoriete boekwinkel.
Daht is main FAH-foh-ree-tuh BOOK-ving-kuhl.

That statue is bigger than it looks.
Dat beeld is groter dan het lijkt.
Daht beylt is GROH-tuhr dahn het laikt.

Look at the shape of that cloud!

Kijk naar de vorm van die wolk!

Kaik nahr duh fohrm fahn dee vohlk!

BUSINESS

I am president of the credit union.
Ik ben voorzitter van de kredietvereniging.
Ik ben FOHR-zi-tuhr fahn duh kre-DEET-vuh-rey-ni-ging.

We are expanding in your area.
We breiden uit in uw regio.
Vuh BRAI-duhn uit in ew REY-gee-oh.

I am looking for work in the agriculture field.
Ik zoek werk in de landbouw.
Ik zook verk in duh LAHNT-bau.

Sign here, please.
Teken hier, alstublieft.
TEY-kuhn heer ahs-too-BLEEFT.

I am looking for temporary work.
Ik zoek tijdelijk werk.
Ik zook TAI-duh-luk verk.

I need to call and set up that meeting.
Ik moet bellen en die vergadering opzetten.
Ik moot BE-luhn en dee fuhr-GAH-duh-ring OHP-ze-tuhn.

Is the line open?
Is de lijn open?
Is duh lain OH-puhn?

I need you to hang up the phone.
Je moet de telefoon ophangen.
Yuh moot duh tey-luh-FOHN OHP-hahng-uhn.

Who should I ask for more information about your business?
Aan wie kan ik meer informatie over uw bedrijf vragen?
Ahn vee kahn ik meyr in-fohr-MAHT-see OH-fuhr ew buh-DRAIF FRAH-guhn?

140

There was no answer when you handed me the phone.
Er was geen antwoord toen je me de telefoon gaf.
Er vahs geyn AHNT-wohrt toon yuh muh duh tey-luh-FOHN gahf.

Robert is not here at the moment.
Robert is hier niet op dit moment.
ROH-buhrt is heer neet ohp dit moh-MENT.

Call me after work, thanks.
Bel me na het werk, bedankt.
Bel muh nah het werk, buh-DAHNKT.

We're strongly considering your contract offer.
We overwegen uw contractaanbieding.
Vuh oh-fuhr-VEY-guhn ew kohn-TRAHKT-ahn-bee-ding.

Have the necessary forms been signed yet?
Zijn de benodigde formulieren al getekend?
Sain duh buh-NOH-dug-duh fohr-moo-LEE-ruhn ahl guh-TEY-kuhnt?

I have a few hours available after work.
Ik heb na het werk een paar uur de tijd.
Ik heb nah het werk uhn pahr oor duh tait.

What do they make there?
Wat maken ze daar?
Vaht MAH-kuhn zuh dahr?

I have no tasks assigned to me.
Ik heb geen taken toegewezen.
Ik heb geyn TAH-kuhn TOO-guh-wey-zuhn.

How many workers are they hiring?
Hoeveel werknemers nemen ze aan?
HOO-feyl VERK-ney-muhrs NEY-muhn zuh ahn?

It should take me three hours to complete this task.
Het zal me waarschijnlijk drie uur kosten om deze taak te voltooien.
Het zahl muh vahr-SGAIN-laik dree oor KOHS-tuhn ohm DEY-zuh tahk tuh fohl-TOH-yuhn.

Don't use that computer, it is only for financial work.
Gebruik die computer niet, die is alleen voor financieel werk.
Guh-BRUIK dee kohm-PYOO-tuhr neet, dee is ah-LEYN fohr fee-nahn-SYEYL verk.

I only employ people that I can rely on.
Ik heb alleen mensen in dienst waar ik op kan vertrouwen.
Ik heb ah-LEYN MEN-suhn in deenst vahr ik ohp kahn fuhr-TRAU-wuhn.

After I talk to my lawyers, we can discuss this further.
Nadat ik met mijn advocaten heb gesproken, kunnen we dit verder
bespreken.
*NAH-daht ik met main aht-voh-KAH-tuhn heb guh-SPROH-kuhn, KUH-nuhn
vuh dit FER-duhr buh-SPREY-kuhn.*

Are there any open positions in my field?
Zijn er vacatures in mijn vakgebied?
Sain er vah-kah-TOO-ruhs in main fahk-guh-BEET?

I'll meet you in the conference room.
Ik zie je in de vergaderruimte.
Ik zee yuh in duh fuhr-GAH-duhr-ruim-tuh.

Call and leave a message on my office phone.
Bel en laat een bericht achter op mijn kantoortelefoon.
Bel en laht uhn buh-RIGT AHG-tuhr ohp main kahn-TOHR-tey-luh-fohn.

Send me a fax with that information.
Stuur me een fax met die informatie.
Stuhr muh uhn fahks met dee in-fohr-MAHT-see.

Hi, I would like to leave a message for Sheila.
Hallo, ik wil een bericht achterlaten voor Sheila.
HAH-loh, ik vil uhn buh-RIGT AHG-tuhr-lah-tuhn fohr shee-lah.

Please repeat your last name.
Herhaal uw achternaam, alstublieft.
Her-HAHL ew AHG-tuhr-nahm, ahs-too-BLEEFT.

I would like to buy wholesale.
Ik wil graag groot inkopen.
Ik vil grahg GROHT in-KOH-puhn.

How do you spell your last name?
Hoe spel je je achternaam?
Hoo spel yuh yuh AHG-tuhr-nahm?

I called your boss yesterday and left a message.
Ik heb gisteren je baas gebeld en een bericht achtergelaten.
Ik heb GIS-tuh-ruhn yuh bahs guh-BELT en uhn buh-RIGT AHG-tuhr-guh-lah-tuhn.

That customer hung up on me.
Die klant hing op.
Dee klahnt hing ohp.

She called but didn't leave a callback number.
Ze belde, maar liet geen nummer achter om terug te bellen.
Zuh BEL-duh, mahr leet geyn NUH-muhr AHG-tuhr ohm tuh-RUG tuh BE-luhn.

Hello! Am I speaking to Bob?
Hallo! Spreek ik met Bob?
HAH-loh! Spreyk ik met bohb?

Excuse me, but could you speak up? I can't hear you.
Pardon, maar kunt u iets harder praten? Ik hoor u niet.
Pahr-DOHN, mahr kuhnt oo eets HAHR-duhr PRAH-tuhn? Ik hohr oo neet.

The line is very bad, could you move to a different area so I can hear you better?
De lijn is erg slecht, kunt u naar een andere plek gaan zodat ik u beter kan horen?
Duh lain is erg slegt, kunt oo nahr uhn AHN-duh-ruh plek gahn ZOH-daht ik oo BEY-tuhr kahn HOH-ruhn?

I would like to apply for a work visa.
Ik wil een werkvisum aanvragen.
Ik vil uhn VERK-fee-suhm AHN-frah-guhn.

It is my dream to work here teaching the language.
Het is mijn droom om hier te werken om anderen de taal te leren.
Het is main drohm ohm heer tuh VER-kuhn ohm AHN-duh-ruhn duh tahl tuh LEY-ruhn.

I have always wanted to work here.
Ik heb hier altijd al willen werken.
Ik heb heer AHL-tait ahl VI-luhn VER-kuhn.

Where do you work?
Waar werk je?
Vahr verk yuh?

Are we in the same field of work?
Zitten we in hetzelfde werkveld?
ZI-tuhn vuh in het-ZELF-duh VERK-felt?

Do we share an office?
Delen we een kantoor?
DEY-luhn vuh uhn kahn-TOHR?

What do you do for a living?
Wat voor werk doe je?
Vaht fohr verk doo yuh?

I work in the city as an engineer for Cosco.
Ik werk in de stad als ingenieur voor Cosco.
Ik verk in duh staht ahls in-zye-NUHR fohr kohs-koh.

I am an elementary teacher.
Ik ben onderwijzer op de basisschool.
Ik ben ohn-der-VAI-zuhr op duh BAH-sis-sgohl.

What time should I be at the meeting?
Hoe laat moet ik bij de vergadering zijn?
Hoo laht moot ik bai duh fuhr-GAH-duh-ring sain?

Would you like me to catch you up on what the meeting was about?
Wil je dat ik je bijpraat over de vergadering?
Vil yuh daht ik yuh BAI-praht OH-fuhr duh fuhr-GAH-duh-ring?

I would like to set up a meeting with your company.
Ik wil graag een afspraak maken met uw bedrijf.
Ik wil grahg uhn AHF-sprahk MAH-kuhn met ew buh-DRAIF.

Please, call my secretary for that information.
Bel mijn secretaresse voor die informatie.
Bel main sey-kruh-tah-RE-suh fohr dee in-fohr-MAHT-see.

I will have to ask my lawyer.
Ik moet het aan mijn advocaat vragen.
Ik moot het ahn main aht-foh-KAHT VRAH-guhn.

144

Fax it over to my office number.
Fax het naar mijn kantoornummer.
Fahks het nahr main kahn-TOHR-nuh-muhr.

Will I have any trouble calling into the office?
Zal ik problemen hebben om naar het kantoor te bellen?
Zahl ik proh-BLEY-muhn HE-buhn ohm nahr het kahn-TOHR tuh BE-luhn?

Do you have a business card I can have?
Heb je een visitekaartje voor mij?
Heb yuh uhn fee-SEE-tuh-kahrt-yuh fohr mai?

Here is my business card. Please, take it.
Hier is mijn visitekaartje. Neem het alstublieft.
Heer is main fee-SEE-tuh-kahrt-yuh. Neym het ahs-too-BLEEFT.

My colleague and I are going to lunch.
Mijn collega en ik gaan lunchen.
Main koh-LEY-gah en ik gahn LUHN-syuhn.

I am the director of finance for my company.
Ik ben de financieel directeur van mijn bedrijf.
Ik ben duh fee-nahn-SYEYL dee-rek-TUHR fahn main buh-DRAIF.

I manage the import goods of my company.
Ik beheer de importgoederen van mijn bedrijf.
Ik buh-HEYR duh IM-pohrt-goo-duh-ruhn fahn main buh-DRAIF.

My colleagues' boss is Steven.
De baas van mijn collega's is Steven.
Duh bahs fahn main koh-LEY-gahs is stey-fuhn.

I work for the gas station company.
Ik werk voor het tankstationbedrijf.
Ik verk fohr het TENK-stah-syohn-buh-draif.

What company do you work for?
Voor welk bedrijf werk je?
Fohr velk buh-DRAIF verk yuh?

I'm an independent contractor.
Ik ben een onafhankelijke contractant.
Ik ben uhn OHN-ahf-hahng-kuh-luh-kuh kohn-trahk-TAHNT.

How many employees do you have at your company?
Hoeveel werknemers heeft u bij uw bedrijf?
HOO-feyl VERK-ney-muhrs heyft oo bai ew buh-DRAIF?

I know a lot about engineering.
Ik weet veel van techniek.
Ik veyt feyl fahn teg-NEEK.

I can definitely resolve that dispute for you.
Ik kan dat geschil zeker voor je oplossen.
Ik kahn daht guh-SGIL ZEY-kuhr fohr yuh OHP-loh-suhn.

You should hire an interpreter.
Je moet een tolk inhuren.
Yuh moot uhn tohlk IN-hew-ruhn.

Are you hiring any additional workers?
Neemt u extra werknemers aan?
Neymt oo EK-strah VERK-ney-muhrs ahn?

How much experience do I need to work here?
Hoeveel ervaring heb ik nodig om hier te werken?
HOO-feyl er-FAH-ring heb ik NOH-duhg ohm heer tuh VER-kuhn?

Our marketing manager handles that.
Onze marketingmanager doet dat.
OHN-zuh MAHR-kuh-ting-me-nuh-guhr doot daht.

I would like to poach one of your workers.
Ik zou één van uw werknemers willen overnemen.
Ik zau eyn fahn ew verk-NEY-muhrs WI-luhn OH-fuhr-ney-muhn.

Can we work out a deal that is beneficial for the both of us?
Kunnen we een deal sluiten die voor ons beiden voordelig is?
KUH-nuhn vuh uhn deel SLUI-tuhn dee fohr ohns BAI-duhn fohr-DEY-luhg is?

My resources are at your disposal.
Mijn middelen staan tot uw beschikking.
Main MI-duh-luhn stahn toht ew buh-SGI-king.

I am afraid that we have to let you go.
Ik ben bang dat we je moeten laten gaan.
Ik ben bahng daht vuh yuh MOO-tuhn LAH-tuhn gahn.

This is your first warning. Please don't do that again.
Dit is je eerste waarschuwing. Doe dat alsjeblieft niet nog een keer.
Dit is yuh EYR-stuh VAHR-sgoo-ving. Doo daht ahs-yuh-BLEEFT neet nohg uhn keyr.

File a complaint with HR about the incident.
Dien een klacht in bij personeelszaken over het incident.
Deen uhn klahgt in bai per-soh-NEYLS-zah-kuhn OH-fuhr het in-see-DENT.

Who is showing up for our lunch meeting?
Wie komt er opdagen voor onze lunchbijeenkomst?
Vee kohmt er OHP-dah-guhn fohr OHN-zuh LUHNSH-bai-eyn-kohmst?

Clear out the rest of my day.
Maak de rest van mijn dag vrij.
Mahk duh rest fahn main dahg frai.

We need to deposit this into the bank.
We moeten dit op de bank storten.
Vuh MOO-tuhn dit ohp duh bahnk STOHR-tuhn.

Can you cover the next hour for me?
Kunt u het volgende uur voor mij invallen?
Kuhnt oo het FOHL-gun-duh oor fohr mai IN-vah-luhn?

If Shania calls, please push her directly through.
Als Shania belt, verbindt haar dan direct door.
Ahls SHAH-nee-ah belt, fuhr-BINT hahr dahn dee-REKT dohr.

I'm leaving early today.
Ik vertrek vandaag vroeg.
Ik fuhr-TREK fahn-DAHG froog.

I'll be working late tonight.
Ik werk vanavond laat.
Ik verk fahn-AH-fohnt laht.

You can use the bathroom in my office.
Je kunt het toilet in mijn kantoor gebruiken.
Yuh kuhnt het twah-LET in main kahn-TOHR guh-BRUI-kuhn.

You can use my office phone to call out.
Je kunt mijn kantoortelefoon gebruiken om naar buiten te bellen.
Yuh kuhnt main kahn-TOHR-tey-luh-fohn guh-BRUI-kuhn ohm nahr BUI-tuhn tuh BE-luhn.

Please, close the door behind you.

Doe alsjeblieft de deur achter je dicht.

Doo ahs-yuh-BLEEFT duh duhr AHG-tuhr yuh digt.

I need to talk to you privately.

Ik moet je persoonlijk spreken.

Ik moot yuh puhr-SOHN-luhk SPREY-kuhn.

Your team is doing good work on this project.

Uw team doet goed werk aan dit project.

Ew teem doot goot verk ahn dit proh-YEKT.

Our numbers are down this quarter.

Onze cijfers zijn dit kwartaal gedaald.

OHN-zuh SAI-fuhrs sain dit kvahr-TAHL guh-DAHLT.

I need you to work harder than usual.

Ik wil dat je harder werkt dan normaal.

Ik vil daht yuh HAHR-duhr verkt dahn nohr-MAHL.

I'm calling in sick today. Can anyone cover my shift?

Ik meld me vandaag ziek. Kan iemand mijn dienst overnemen?

Ik melt muh fahn-DAHG zeek. Kahn EE-mahnt main deenst OH-fuhr-ney-muhn?

Tom, we are thinking of promoting you.

Tom, we denken erover je promotie te geven.

Tohm, vuh DENG-kuhn er-OH-fuhr yuh proh-MOHT-see tuh GEY-fuhn.

I would like a raise.

Ik wil graag een loonsverhoging.

Ik vil grahg uhn LOHNS-fuhr-hoh-ging.

THE WEATHER

I think the weather is changing.
Ik denk dat het weer aan het veranderen is.
Ik denk daht het veyr ahn het fuhr-AHN-duh-ruhn is.

Be careful, it is raining outside.
Wees voorzichtig, het regent buiten.
Veys fohr-ZIG-tig, het REY-guhnt BUI-tuhn.

Make sure to bring your umbrella.
Zorg ervoor dat je je paraplu meeneemt.
Zohrg er-FOHR daht yuh yuh pah-rah-PLOO MEY-neymt.

Get out of the rain or you will catch a cold.
Kom uit de regen of je wordt verkouden.
Kohm uit duh REY-guhn ohf yuh vohrt fuhr-KAU-duhn.

Is it snowing?
Sneeuwt het?
Sneywt het?

The snow is very thick right now.
De sneeuw is momenteel erg dik.
Duh sneyw is moh-muhn-TEYL erg dik.

Be careful, the road is full of ice.
Wees voorzichtig, de weg ligt vol met ijs.
Veys fohr-ZIG-tig, duh weg ligt fohl met ais.

What is the climate like here? Is it warm or cold?
Hoe is het klimaat hier? Is het warm of koud?
Hoo is het klee-MAHT heer? Is het vahrm ohf kaut?

It has been a very nice temperature here.
Het is hier een erg aangename temperatuur geweest.
Het is heer uhn erg AHN-guh-nah-muh tem-puh-rah-TOOR guh-VEYST.

Does it rain a lot here?
Regent het hier veel?
REY-guhnt het heer feyl?

The temperature is going to break records this week.
De temperatuur gaat deze week records breken.
Duh tem-puh-rah-TUHR gaht DEY-zuh veyk ruh-KOHRS BREY-kuhn.

Does it ever snow here?
Sneeuwt het hier ooit?
Sneywt het heer ooeet?

When does it get sunny?
Wanneer wordt het zonnig?
Vah-NEYR vohrt het ZOH-nuhg?

What's the forecast look like for tomorrow?
Hoe ziet de voorspelling voor morgen eruit?
Hoo zeet duh fohr-SPE-ling fohr MOHR-guhn ER-uit?

This is a heatwave.
Dit is een hittegolf.
Dit is uhn HI-tuh-gohlf.

Right now, it is overcast, but it should clear up by this evening.
Op dit moment is het bewolkt, maar het zou vanavond moeten zijn
opgehelderd.
Op dit moh-MENT is het buh-VOHLKT, mahr het zau fahn-AH-fohnt MOO-
tuhn sain OHP-guh-hel-duhrt.

It is going to heat up in the afternoon.
Het wordt 's middags warm.
Het vohrt SMI-dahgs vahrm.

What channel is the weather channel?
Welk kanaal is het weerkanaal?
Velk kah-NAHL is het VEYR-kah-nahl?

Tonight it will be below freezing.
Vanavond zal het onder het vriespunt zijn.
Fahn-AH-fohnt zahl het OHN-duhr het FREES-puhnt sain.

It's very windy outside.
Het is erg winderig buiten.
Het is erg VIN-duh-ruhg BUI-tuhn.

It's going to be cold in the morning.
Het wordt 's ochtends koud.
Het vohrt SOHG-tuhnds kaut.

It's not raining, only drizzling.
Het regent niet, het miezert alleen.
Het REY-guhnt neet, het MEE-zuhrt ah-LEYN.

HOTEL

I would like to book a room.
Ik wil graag een kamer boeken.
Ik vil grahg uhn KAH-muhr BOO-kuhn.

I'd like a single room.
Ik wil een eenpersoonskamer.
Ik vil uhn EYN-puhr-sohns-KAH-muhr.

I'd like a suite.
Ik wil een suite.
Ik vil uhn sweet.

How much is the room per night?
Hoeveel kost de kamer per nacht?
HOO-feyl kohst duh KAH-muhr per nahgt?

How much is the room with tax?
Hoeveel kost de kamer met belasting?
HOE-feyl kohst duh KAH-mur met buh-LAHS-ting?

When is the checkout time?
Wanneer is de uitchecktijd?
Vah-NEYR is duh UIT-tyek-tait?

I'd like a room with a nice view.
Ik wil een kamer met mooi uitzicht.
Ik vil uhn KAH-muhr met mohee UIT-zigt.

I'd like to order room service.
Ik wil roomservice bestellen.
Ik vil ROOM-suhr-fis buh-STE-luhn.

Let's go swim in the outdoor pool.
Laten we gaan zwemmen in het buitenzwembad.
Laten vuh gahn ZVE-muhn in het BUI-tuhn-zvem-baht.

Are pets allowed at the hotel?
Zijn huisdieren toegestaan in het hotel?
Sain HUIS-dee-ruhn TOO-guh-stahn in het hoh-TEL?

I would like a room on the first floor.
Ik wil graag een kamer op de eerste verdieping.
Ik vil grahg uhn KAH-muhr ohp duh EYR-stuh fuhr-DEE-ping.

Can you send maintenance up to our room for a repair?
Kunt u de technische dienst naar onze kamer sturen voor een reparatie?
Kuhnt oo duh TEG-nee-se-deenst nahr OHN-zuh KAH-muhr STOO-ruhn fohr uhn rey-pah-RAHT-see?

I'm locked out of my room, could you unlock it?
Ik ben buitengesloten uit mijn kamer, kun je de deur openen?
Ik ben BUI-tuhn-guh-sloh-tun uit main KAH-muhr, kuhn yuh duh duhr OH-puh-nuhn?

Our door is jammed and won't open.
Onze deur zit vast en gaat niet open.
OHN-zuh duhr zit fahst en gaht neet OH-puhn.

How do you work the shower?
Hoe bedien je de douche?
Hoo buh-DEEN yuh duh doosh?

Are the consumables in the room free?
Zijn de verbruiksartikelen in de kamer gratis?
Sain duh fuhr-BRUIKS-ahr-tee-kuh-luhn in duh KAH-muhr GRAH-tis?

What is my final bill for the stay, including incidentals?
Wat is mijn eindfactuur voor het verblijf, inclusief incidentele kosten?
Vaht is main EINT-fahk-tuhr fohr het fuhr-BLAIF, IN-kloo-seef in-see-den-TEY-luh KOHS-tuhn?

Can you show me to my room?
Kun je me naar mijn kamer brengen?
Kuhn yuh muh nahr main KAH-muhr BRENG-uhn?

Where can I get ice for my room?
Waar kan ik ijs voor mijn kamer krijgen?
Vahr kahn ik ais fohr main KAH-muhr KRAI-guhn?

Do you have any rooms available?
Heeft u kamers beschikbaar?
Heyft oo KAH-muhrs buh-SGIK-bahr?

Do you sell bottled water?
Verkoopt u flessen water?
Fuhr-KOHPT oo FLE-suhn VAH-tuhr?

Our towels are dirty.
Onze handdoeken zijn vies.
OHN-zuh HAGN-doo-kuhn sain fees.

Have you stayed at this hotel before?
Heb je eerder in dit hotel overnacht?
Heb yuh EYR-duhr in dit hoh-TEL OH-fuhr-nahgt?

How much is a room for two adults?
Hoeveel kost een kamer voor twee volwassenen?
HOO-feyl kohst uhn KAH-muhr fohr tvey vohl-VAH-suh-nuhn?

Does the room come with a microwave?
Is de kamer voorzien van een magnetron?
Is duh KAH-muhr fohr-ZEEN fahn uhn mahg-nuh-TROHN?

May I see the room first? That way I will know if I like it.
Mag ik eerst de kamer zien? Op die manier weet ik of ik hem mooi vind.
Mahg ik eyrst duh KAH-muhr zeen? Ohp dee mah-NEER veyt ik ohf ik hem mohee fint.

Do you have a room that is quieter?
Heeft u een kamer die stiller is?
Heyft oo uhn KAH-muhr dee RUHS-ti-guhr is?

How much is the deposit for my stay?
Hoeveel bedraagt de aanbetaling voor mijn verblijf?
HOO-feyl buh-DRAHGT duh AHN-buh-tah-ling fohr main fuhr-BLAIF?

Is the tap water drinkable at the hotel?
Is het kraanwater drinkbaar in het hotel?
Is het KRAHN-vah-tuhr DRINK-bahr in het hoh-TEL?

Will there be any holds on my credit card?
Worden er reserveringen op mijn creditcard geboekt?
VOHR-duhn er rey-ser-FEY-ring-uhn op mijn KRE-dit-card guh-BOOKT?

Can I get a replacement room key?
Kan ik een vervangende kamersleutel krijgen?
Kahn ik uhn fuhr-FAHNG-uhn-duh KAH-muhr-sluh-tuhl KRAI-guhn?

How much is a replacement room key?
Hoeveel kost een vervangende kamersleutel?
HOO-feyl kohst uhn fuhr-FAHNG-uhn-duh KAH-muhr-sluh-tuhl?

Does the bathroom have a shower or a bathtub?
Heeft de badkamer een douche of een bad?
Heyft duh BAHT-kah-muhr uhn doosh ohf uhn baht?

Are any of the channels on the TV available in English?
Zijn de kanalen op de tv in het Engels beschikbaar?
Sain duh kah-NAH-luhn ohp duh tey-fey in het ENG-uhls buh-SGIK-bahr?

I want a bigger room.
Ik wil een grotere kamer.
Ik vil uhn GROH-tuh-ruh KAH-muhr.

Do you serve breakfast in the morning?
Serveert u 's ochtends ontbijt?
Ser-FEYRT oo SOHG-tuhnds ohnt-BAIT?

Oh, it's spacious.
Oh, het is groot.
Oh, het is groht.

My room is this way.
Mijn kamer is deze kant op.
Main KAH-muhr is DEY-zuh kahnt ohp.

Straight down the hall.
Rechtdoor tot het eind van de gang.
Regtdoor toht het aint fahn duh gahng.

Can you suggest a different hotel?
Kunt u een ander hotel aanbevelen?
Kuhnt oo uhn AHN-duhr hoh-TEL AHN-buh-fey-luhn?

Does the room have a safe for my valuables?
Heeft de kamer een kluis voor mijn waardevolle spullen?
Heyft duh KAH-muhr uhn kluis fohr main VAHR-duh-voh-luh SPUH-luhn?

Please clean my room.
Maak alstublieft mijn kamer schoon.
Mahk ahs-too-BLEEFT main KAH-muhr sgohn.

Don't disturb me, please.
Stoor me alstublieft niet.
Stohr muh ahs-too-BLEEFT neet.

Can you wake me up at noon?
Kunt u me om twaalf uur 's middags wakker maken?
Kuhnt oo muh ohm tvahlf oor SMI-dahgs WAH-kuhr MAH-kuhn?

I would like to check out of my hotel room.
Ik wil graag uitchecken uit mijn hotelkamer.
Ik vil grahg UIT-che-kuhn uit main hoh-TEL-kah-muhr.

Please increase the cleanup duty of my hotel room.
Maak alstublieft mijn hotelkamer vaker schoon.
Mahk ahs-too-BLEEFT main hoh-TEL-kah-muhr FAH-kuhr sgohn.

Is the Marriott any good?
Is het Marriott goed?
Is het Marriott goot?

Is it expensive to stay at the Marriott?
Is het duur om in het Marriott te overnachten?
Is het duhr ohm in het Marriot tuh OH-fuhr-nahgt-uhn?

I think our room has bedbugs.
Ik denk dat onze kamer bedwantsen heeft.
Ik denk daht OHN-zuh KAH-muhr BET-vahnt-suhn heyft.

Can you send an exterminator to our room?
Kunt u een verdelger naar onze kamer sturen?
Kuhnt oo uhn fuhr-DEL-guhr nahr OHN-zuh KAH-muhr STOO-ruhn?

I need to speak to your manager.
Ik moet je manager spreken.
Ik moot yuh ME-nuh-dyur SPREY-kuhn.

Do you have the number to corporate?
Heeft u het zakelijke nummer?
Heyft oo het ZAH-kuh-luh-kuh NUH-muhr?

Does the hotel shuttle go to the casino?
Gaat de hotelshuttle naar het casino?
Gaht duh hoh-TEL-shuh-tuhl nahr het kah-SEE-no?

Can you call me when the hotel shuttle is on its way?
Kun je me bellen als de hotelshuttle onderweg is?
Kuhn yuh muh BE-luhn ahls duh hoh-TEL-shuh-tuhl ohn-duhr-WEG is?

Can we reserve this space for a party?
Kunnen we deze ruimte reserveren voor een feestje?
KUH-nuhn vuh DEY-zuh RUIM-tuh rey-suhr-FEY-ruhn fohr uhn FEYST-yuh?

What is the guest limit for reserving an area?
Wat is de gastlimiet voor het reserveren van een plaats?
Vaht is duh GAHST-lee-meet fohr het rey-suhr-FEY-ruhn fahn uhn plahts?

What are the rules for reserving an area?
Wat zijn de regels voor het reserveren van een plaats?
Vaht sain duh REY-guhls fohr het rey-suhr-FEY-ruhn fahn uhn plahts?

Can we serve or drink alcohol during our get together?
Kunnen we tijdens onze bijeenkomst alcohol serveren of drinken?
KUH-nuhn vuh TAI-duhns OHN-zuh bai-EYN-kohmst AHL-koh-hol ser-FEY-ruhn ohf DRINK-uhn?

I would like to complain about a noisy room next to us.
Ik zou willen klagen over een luidruchtige kamer naast ons.
Ik zau WI-luhn KLAH-guhn OH-fuhr uhn luit-RUHG-tuh-guh KAH-muhr nahst ohns.

We have some personal items missing from our room.
Er missen enkele persoonlijke bezittingen uit onze kamer.
Er MI-suhn ENG-kuh-luh puhr-SOHN-luh-kuh buh-ZI-ting-uhn uit OHN-zuh KAH-muhr.

SPORTS AND EXERCISE

Can we walk faster?

Kunnen we sneller lopen?

KUH-nuhn vuh SNE-luhr LOH-puhn?

Do you want to go to a drag race track?

Wil je naar een drag-racebaan gaan?

Vil yuh nahr uhn DREG-reys-bahn gahn?

Are you taking a walk?

Ga je wandelen?

Ga yuh VAHN-duh-luhn?

Do you want to jog for a kilometer or two?

Wil je een kilometer of twee joggen?

Vil yuh uhn KEE-loh-mey-tuhr ohf tvey DYOH-guhn?

How about fast walking?

Wat dacht je van snelwandelen?

Vaht dahgt yuh fahn SNEL-vahn-duh-luhn?

Would you like to walk with me?

Wil je met me wandelen?

Vil yuh met muh VAHN-duh-luhn?

He is a really good player.

Hij is een heel goede speler.

Hai is uhn heyl GOO-duh SPEY-luhr.

I feel bad that they traded him to the other team.

Ik vind het erg dat ze hem aan het andere team hebben verkocht.

Ik fint het erg daht zuh hem ahn het AHN-duh-ruh teem HE-buhn fehr-KOHGT.

Did you see that home run?

Heb je die homerun gezien?

Heb yuh dee homerun guh-ZEEN?

I have been a fan of that team for many years.
Ik ben al jaren fan van dat team.
Ik ben ahl JAH-ruhn fen fahn daht teem.

Who is your favorite team?
Wat is je favoriete team?
Vat is yuh FAH-foh-ree-tuh teem?

Pelé is my favorite player.
Pelé is mijn favoriete speler.
Pe-LEY is main fah-foh-REE-tuh SPEY-luhr.

Do you like soccer?
Vind je voetbal leuk?
Fint yuh FOOT-bahl luhk?

Do you watch American football?
Kijk je naar American football?
Kaik yuh nahr ah-me-ri-kahn football?

Are there any games on right now?
Zijn er momenteel wedstrijden te zien?
Sain er moh-men-TEYL WET-strai-duhn tuh zeen?

That was a bad call by the ref.
Dat was een slechte beslissing van de scheidsrechter.
Daht vahs uhn SLEG-tuh buh-SLI-sing fahn duh SGEITS-reg-tuhr.

I put a lot of money on this game.
Ik heb veel geld gestoken in dit spel.
Ik heb feyl gelt guh-STOH-kuhn in dit spel.

His stats have been incredible this season.
Zijn statistieken waren dit seizoen ongelooflijk.
Sain staht-tis-TEE-kuhn WAH-ruhn dit sai-ZOON ohn-guh-LOH-fuh-luk.

Do you want to play baseball today?
Wil je vandaag honkbal spelen?
Vil yuh fahn-DAHG HOHNK-bahl SPEY-luhn?

Let's go to the soccer field and practice.
Laten we naar het voetbalveld gaan en oefenen.
LAH-tuhn vuh nahr het FOOT-bahl-velt gahn en OO-fuh-nuhn.

I am barely working up a sweat.
Ik zweet nauwelijks.
Ik zveyt NAU-vuh-luhks.

Let's go to the gym and lift weights.
Laten we naar de sportschool gaan en gewichten heffen.
LA-tuhn vuh nahr duh SPOHRT-sgohl gahn en guh-WIG-tuhn HE-fuhn.

Give me more weights.
Geef me meer gewichten.
Geyf muh meyr guh-WIG-tuhn.

Take some weights off.
Doe er wat gewichten af.
Doo er vaht guh-WIG-tuhn ahf.

Will you spot me?
Wil je me spotten?
Vil yuh muh SPO-tuhn?

How long do you want to run on the treadmill?
Hoe lang wil je hardlopen op de loopband?
Hoo lahng vil yuh HAHRT-loh-puhn ohp duh LOHP-bahnt?

Is this the best gym in the area?
Is dit de beste sportschool in de buurt?
Is dit duh BES-tuh SPOHRT-sgohl in duh buhrt?

Do I need a membership to enter this gym?
Heb ik een lidmaatschap nodig om deze sportschool binnen te gaan?
Heb ik uhn LIT-maht-sgahp NOH-duhg ohm DEY-zuh SPOHRT-sgohl BI-nuhn tuh gahn?

Do you have trial memberships for tourists?
Heeft u proeflidmaatschappen voor toeristen?
Heyft oo PROOF-lit-maht-sgah-puhn fohr too-RIS-tuhn?

My muscles are still sore from the last workout.
Mijn spieren doen nog pijn van de laatste training.
Main SPEE-ruhn doon nohg pain fahn duh LAHT-stuh TREY-ning.

Give me a second while I adjust this.
Geef me een momentje terwijl ik dit aanpas.
Geyf muh uhn moh-MENT-yuh tuhr-WAIL ik dit AHN-pahs.

Time to hit the steam room!
Tijd om naar het stoombad te gaan!
Tait ohm nahr het STOHM-baht tuh gahn!

You can put that in my locker.
Je kunt dat in mijn kluisje stoppen.
Yuh kuhnt daht in main KLUIS-yuh STOH-puhn.

I think we have to take turns on this machine.
Ik denk dat we dit toestel om de beurt moeten gebruiken.
Ik denk daht vuh dit TOO-stel ohm duh buhrt MOO-tuhn guh-BRUI-kuhn.

Make sure to wipe down the equipment when you are done.
Zorg ervoor dat je de apparatuur afveegt als je klaar bent.
Zohrg er-FOHR daht yuh duh ah-pah-rah-TOOR AHF-feygt ahls yuh klahr bent.

Is there a time limit on working out here?
Is er een tijdslimiet om hier te trainen?
Is er uhn TAITS-lee-meet ohm heer tuh TREY-nuhn?

We should enter a marathon.
We moeten aan een marathon deelnemen.
Vuh MOO-tuhn ahn uhn mah-rah-TOHN DEYL-ney-muhn.

How has your diet been going?
Hoe gaat het met je dieet?
Hoo gaht het met yuh dee-YEET?

Are you doing keto?
Doe je keto?
Doo yuh KE-toh?

Make sure to stay hydrated while you work out.
Zorg ervoor dat je tijdens het sporten gehydrateerd blijft.
Zohrg er-FOHR daht yuh TAI-duhns het SPOHR-tuhn guh-hee-drah-TEYRT blaift.

I'll go grab you a protein shake.
Ik ga een eiwitshake voor je halen.
Ik gah uhn AI-vit-sheyk fohr yuh HAH-luhn.

Do you want anything else? I'm buying.
Wil je nog iets anders? Ik trakteer.
Vil yuh nohg eets AHN-duhrs? Ik trahk-TEYR.

I need to buy some equipment before I play that.
Ik moet wat apparatuur kopen voordat ik dat speel.
Ik moot vaht ah-pah-rah-TUHR KOH-puhn FOHR-daht ik daht speyl.

Do you want to spar?
Wil je sparren?
Vil yuh SPAH-ruhn?

Full contact sparring.
Full contact sparring.
Full contact sparring.

Just a simple practice round.
Gewoon een simpele oefenronde.
Guh-VOHN uhn SIM-puh-luh OO-fuhn-rohn-duh.

Do you want to wrestle?
Wil je worstelen?
Vil yuh VOHR-stuh-luhn?

What are the rules to play this game?
Wat zijn de regels om dit spel te spelen?
Vaht sain duh REY-guhls ohm dit spel tuh SPEY-luhn?

Do we need a referee?
Hebben we een scheidsrechter nodig?
HE-buhn vuh uhn SGEITS-reg-tuhr NOH-duhg?

I don't agree with that call.
Ik ben het niet eens met die beslissing.
Ik ben het neet eyns met dee buh-SLI-sing.

Can we get another opinion on that score?
Kunnen we een andere mening krijgen over die score?
KUH-nuhn vuh uhn AHN-duh-ruh MEY-ning KRAI-guhn OH-fuhr dee SKOH-ruh?

How about a game of table tennis?
Wat dacht je van een potje tafeltennis?
Vaht dahgt yuh fahn uhn POHT-yuh TAH-fuhl-te-nis?

Do you want to team up?
Wil je samen in een team spelen?
Vil yuh SAH-muhn in uhn tem SPEY-luhn?

Goal!
Goal!
Goal!

Homerun!
Homerun!
Home-RUN!

Touchdown!
Touchdown!
TOUCH-down!

Score!
Score!
Score!

On your mark, get set, go!
Op je plaats, klaar, af!
Ohp yuh plahts, klahr, ahf!

Do you want to borrow my equipment?
Wil je mijn uitrusting lenen?
Vil yuh main UIT-ruhs-ting LEY-nuhn?

Hold the game for a second.
Leg de wedstrijd even stil.
Leg duh WET-strait EY-fuhn stil.

I don't understand the rules of this game.
Ik begrijp de regels van dit spel niet.
Ik buh-GRAIP duh REY-guhls fahn DEY-zuh WET-strait neet.

Timeout!
Time-out!
Time out!

Can we switch sides?
Kunnen we van kant wisselen?
KUH-nuhn vuh fahn kahnt VI-suh-luhn?

There is something wrong with my equipment.
Er is iets mis met mijn uitrusting.
Er is eets mis met main UIT-ruhs-ting.

How about another game?
Wat dacht je van nog een wedstrijd?
Vaht dahgt yuh fahn nohg uhn WET-strait?

I would like a do over of that last game.
Ik zou graag die laatste wedstrijd willen overdoen.
Ik zau grahg dee LAHT-stuh WET-strait VI-lun OH-fuhr-doon.

Do want to go golfing?
Wil je gaan golfen?
Vil yuh gahn GOHL-fuhn?

Where can we get a golf cart?
Waar kunnen we een golfkar krijgen?
Vahr KUH-nuhn vuh uhn GOHLF-kahr KRAI-guhn?

Do you have your own clubs?
Heeft u uw eigen clubs?
Heyft oo ew AI-guhn clubs?

Would you like to play with my spare clubs?
Wil je spelen met mijn reserveclubs?
Vil yuh SPEY-luhn met main ruh-SER-vuh-clubs?

How many holes do you want to play?
Hoeveel holes wil je spelen?
HOO-feyl holes vil yuh SPEY-luhn?

Do I have to be a member of this club to play?
Moet ik lid zijn van deze club om te spelen?
Moot ik lit sain fahn DEY-zuh cluhb ohm tuh SPEY-luhn?

Let me ice this down, it is sore.
Laat me hier ijs op doen, het is pijnlijk.
Laht muh heer ais ohp doon, het is PAIN-luhk.

I can't keep up with you, slow down.
Ik kan je niet bijhouden, ga wat langzamer.
Ik kahn yuh neet BAI-hau-duhn, gah vaht LAHNG-sah-muhr.

Let's pick up the pace a little bit.
Laten we het tempo een beetje opvoeren.
LAH-tuhn vuh het TEM-poh uhn BEYT-yuh OHP-foo-ruhn.

Do you need me to help you with that?
Moet ik je daarbij helpen?
Moot ik yuh DAHR-bai HEL-puhn?

Am I being unfair?
Ben ik oneerlijk?
Ben ik ohn-EYR-luhk?

Let's switch teams for the next game.
Laten we van team wisselen voor de volgende wedstrijd.
LAH-tuhn vuh fahn teem VI-suh-luhn fohr duh FOHL-guhn-duh WET-strait.

Hand me those weights.
Geef me die gewichten aan.
Geyf muh dee guh-WIG-tuhn ahn.

THE FIRST 24 HOURS AFTER ARRIVING

When did you arrive?
Wanneer ben je aangekomen?
Vah-NEYR ben yuh AHN-guh-koh-muhn?

That was a very pleasant flight.
Dat was een erg prettige vlucht.
Daht vahs uhn erg PRE-tuh-guh vluhgt.

Yes, it was a very peaceful trip. Nothing bad happened.
Ja, het was een heel rustige reis. Er is niets ergs gebeurd.
Yah, het vahs uhn heyl RUHS-tuh-guh rais. Er is neets ergs guh-BUHRT.

I have jetlag so need to lay down for a bit.
Ik heb een jetlag, dus ik moet even gaan liggen.
Ik heb uhn DYET-leg, duhs ik moot EY-fuhn gahn LI-guhn.

No, that was my first time flying.
Nee, dat was mijn eerste keer vliegen.
Ney, daht vahs main EYR-stuh keyr FLEE-guhn.

When is the check-in time?
Wanneer is de inchecktijd?
Vah-NEYR is duh IN-chek-tait?

Do we need to get cash?
Moeten we contant geld halen?
MOO-tuhn vuh kohn-TAHNT gelt HAH-luhn?

How much money do you have on you?
Hoeveel geld heb je bij je?
HOO-feyl gelt heb yuh bai yuh?

How long do you want to stay here?
Hoe lang wil je hier blijven?
Hoo lahng vil yuh heer BLAI-fuhn?

Do we have all of our luggage?
Hebben we al onze bagage?
HE-buhn vuh ahl OHN-zuh bah-GAH-syuh?

Let's walk around the city a bit before checking in.
Laten we een beetje door de stad lopen voordat we inchecken.
LAH-tuhn vuh uhn BEYT-yuh dohr duh staht LOH-puhn FOHR-daht vuh IN-che-kuhn.

When is check-in time for our hotel?
Wanneer is de inchecktijd voor ons hotel?
Vah-NEYR is duh IN-chek-tait fohr ohns hoh-TEL?

I'll call the landlord and let him know we landed.
Ik bel de eigenaar en laat hem weten dat we zijn geland.
Ik bel duh AI-guh-nahr en laht hem WEY-tuhn dat vuh sain guh-LAHNT.

Let's find a place to rent a car.
Laten we een plek zoeken om een auto te huren.
LAH-tuhn vuh uhn plek ZOO-kuhn ohm uhn AU-toh tuh HEW-ruhn.

Let's walk around the hotel room and make sure it's correct.
Laten we door de hotelkamer lopen en controleren of deze in orde is.
LAH-tuhn vuh dohr duh hoh-TEL-kah-muhr LOH-puhn en kohn-troh-LEY-ruhn ohf DEY-zuh in OHR-duh is.

We'll look at our apartment and make sure everything is in order.
We zullen naar ons appartement kijken en ervoor zorgen dat alles in orde is.
Vuh ZUH-luhn nahr ohns ah-pahr-tuh-MENT KAI-kuhn en er-FOHR ZOHR-guhn daht AH-luhs in OHR-duh is.

THE LAST 24 HOURS BEFORE LEAVING

Where are the passports?
Waar zijn de paspoorten?
Vahr sain duh PAHS-pohr-tuhn?

Did you fill out the customs forms?
Heeft u de douaneformulieren ingevuld?
Heyft oo duh doo-AH-nuh-for-moo-lee-ruhn IN-guh-fuhlt?

Make sure to pack everything.
Zorg ervoor dat je alles inpakt.
Zohrg er-FOHR daht yuh AH-lus IN-pahkt.

Where are we going?
Waar gaan we naartoe?
Vahr gahn vuh nahr-TOO?

Which flight are we taking?
Welke vlucht nemen we?
VEL-kuh fluhgt NEY-muhn vuh?

Check your pockets.
Controleer je zakken.
Kohn-troh-LEYR yuh ZAH-kuhn.

I need to declare some things for customs.
Ik moet wat dingen aangeven voor de douane.
Ik moot vaht DING-uhn AHN-gey-fuhn fohr duh doo-AH-nuh.

No, I have nothing to declare.
Nee, ik heb niets aan te geven.
Ney, ik heb neets ahn tuh GEY-fuhn.

What is the checkout time?
Wat is de uitchecktijd?
Vaht is duh UIT-chek-tait?

Make sure your phone is charged.
Zorg ervoor dat je telefoon is opgeladen.
Zohrg er-FOHR daht yuh tey-luh-FOHN is OHP-guh-lah-duhn.

Is there a fee attached to this?
Zijn hier kosten aan verbonden?
Sain heer KOHS-tuhn ahn fuhr-BOHN-duhn?

Do we have any outstanding bills to pay?
Moeten we nog openstaande rekeningen betalen?
MOO-tuhn vuh nohg OH-puhn-stahn-duh REY-kuh-ning-uhn buh-TAH-luhn?

What time does our flight leave?
Hoe laat vertrekt onze vlucht?
Hoo laht fuhr-TREKT OHN-zuh vluhgt?

What time do we need to be in the airport?
Hoe laat moeten we op de luchthaven zijn?
Hoo laht MOO-tuhn vuh ohp duh LUHGT-hah-fuhn sain?

How bad is the traffic going in the direction of the airport?
Hoe druk is het verkeer in de richting van de luchthaven?
Hoo druhk is het fer-KEYR in duh RIG-ting fahn duh LUHGT-hah-fuhn?

Are there any detours we can take?
Zijn er andere routes die we kunnen nemen?
Sain er AHN-duh-ruh dee vuh KUH-nuhn NEY-muhn?

What haven't we seen from our list since we've been down here?
Wat hebben we niet van onze lijst gezien sinds we hier zijn?
Vaht HE-buhn vuh neet fahn OHN-zuh laist guh-ZEEN sints vuh hier zijn?

We should really buy some souvenirs here.
We moeten hier echt wat souvenirs kopen.
Vuh MOO-tuhn heer egt vaht soo-vuh-NEERS KOH-puhn.

Do you know any shortcuts that will get us there faster?
Kent u binnendoorwegen die ons er sneller brengen?
Kent oo bi-nuhn-DOHR-WEY-guhn dee ohns er SNE-luhr BRENG-uhn?

GPS the location and save it.
Bepaal de gps-coördinaten en sla ze op.
Buh-PAAL duh Gey-pey-ES KO-ohr-di-nah-ten en slah zuh ohp.

169

Are the items we're bringing back allowed on the plane?
Zijn de spullen die we meenemen toegestaan in het vliegtuig?
Sain duh SPUH-luhn dee vuh mey-MEH-muhn TOO-guh-stahn in het FLEEG-tuig?

We should call our family back home before leaving.
We moeten onze familie thuis bellen voordat we vertrekken.
Vuh MOO-tuhn OHN-zuh fah-MEE-lee tuis BE-luhn FOHR-daht vuh fuhr-TRE-kuhn.

Make sure the pet cage is locked.
Zorg ervoor dat de huisdieren-kooi op slot zit.
Zohrg er-FOHR daht duh HUIS-dee-ruhn kohee ohp sloht zit.

Go through your luggage again.
Ga nog een keer door je bagage.
Gah nohg uhn keyr dohr yuh bah-gah-syuh.

CONCLUSION

Congratulations! You have reached the end of this book and learned over **1,500** ways to express yourself in the Dutch language! It is a moment to celebrate, since you are now much closer to achieving complete fluency of the Dutch tongue.

However, the learning simply cannot end here – you may have unlocked a massive amount of incredibly useful day-to-day phrases that will get you anywhere you need to go, but are you prepared to use them correctly? Furthermore, will you actually remember them during your travels when faced with one of the situations we've presented in this book?

Only by continuously studying the material found in these chapters will you ever be able to summon the words and phrases encountered above, since it isn't a matter of *what* the phrases are but *how* and *when* to use them. Knowing the exact context is crucial, as well as reinforcing your knowledge with other materials.

For this reason, we have created a quick list of tips to make the most of this Dutch Phrasebook and expanding your vocabulary and grasp of the Dutch language:

1. **Practice every day:** You can be very good at something thanks to the gift of natural talent, but practice is the only way to *stay* good. Make sure to constantly pick up the book and read the words, saying them out loud and taking note of your mistakes so you can correct them.

2. **Read while listening:** A very popular and modern way of learning a new language is by using the RWL (reading while listening) method. It has been proven that this method can greatly boost fluency, help you ace language tests, and improve your learning in other subjects. Feel free to try out our audiobooks and other listening materials in Dutch – you'll love them!

3. **Studying in groups:** It's always best to go on an adventure together – even if it's a language adventure! You'll enjoy yourself more if you can find someone who wants to learn with you. Look to friends, your partner, your family members, or colleagues for support, and maybe they can even help you make the process easier and quicker!

4. **Creating your own exercises:** This book provides you with plenty of material for your learning processes, and you will probably be happy with reading it every time you can…however, you need to increase the difficulty by looking for other words and phrases in the Dutch language which you don't know the pronunciation to and trying to decipher them for yourself. Use the knowledge you've gained with previous lessons to discover entirely new words!

With that said, we have now fully concluded this Dutch Phrasebook, which will surely accelerate your learning to new levels. Don't forget to follow every tip we've included and keep an eye out for our additional Dutch materials.

MORE BOOKS BY LINGO MASTERY

Have you been trying to learn Dutch and simply can't find the way to expand your vocabulary?

Do your teachers recommend you boring textbooks and complicated stories that you don't really understand?

Are you looking for a way to learn the language quicker without taking shortcuts?

If you answered *"Yes!"* to at least one of those previous questions, then this book is for you! We've compiled the **2000 Most Common Words in Dutch,** a list of terms that will expand your vocabulary to levels previously unseen.

Did you know that — according to an important study — learning the top two thousand (2000) most frequently used words will enable you to understand up to **84%** of all non-fiction and **86.1%** of fiction literature and **92.7%** of oral speech? Those are *amazing* stats, and this book will take you even further than those numbers!

In this book:

- A detailed introduction with tips and tricks on how to improve your learning

- A list of **2000** of the most common words in Dutch and their translations
- An example sentence for each word – in both Dutch *and* English
- Finally, a conclusion to make sure you've learned and supply you with a final list of tips

Don't look any further, we've got what you need right here!

In fact, we're ready to turn you into a Dutch speaker... are you ready to become one?

DUTCH
SHORT STORIES
FOR BEGINNERS

20 CAPTIVATING SHORT STORIES TO LEARN DUTCH AND GROW
YOUR VOCABULARY THE FUN WAY!

Lingo Mastery

Do you know what the hardest thing for a Dutch learner is?

Finding *PROPER* reading material that they can handle...which is precisely the reason we've written this book!

Teachers love giving out tough, expert-level literature to their students. Books that present many new problems to the reader and force them to search for words in a dictionary every five minutes — it's not entertaining, useful or motivating for the student at all, and many soon give up on learning at all!

In this book, we have compiled 20 easy-to-read, compelling and fun stories that will allow you to expand your vocabulary and give you the tools to improve your grasp of the beautiful Dutch tongue.

How **Dutch Short Stories for Beginners** works:

- Each story is exciting and entertaining with realistic dialogues and day-to-day situations.
- The summaries follow a synopsis in Dutch and in English of what you just read, both to review the lesson and for you to see if you understood what the tale was about.
- At the end of those summaries, you'll be provided with a list of the most relevant vocabulary involved in the lesson, as well as slang and sayings that you may not have understood at first glance!

- Finally, you'll be provided with a set of tricky questions in Dutch, providing you with the chance to prove that you learned something in the story. Don't worry if you don't know the answer to any — we will provide them immediately after, but no cheating!

We want you to feel comfortable while learning the tongue; after all, no language should be a barrier for you to travel around the world and expand your social circles!

So look no further! Pick up your copy of **Dutch Short Stories for Beginners** and start learning Dutch *right now*!

OVER 100 DUTCH CONVERSATIONS AND SHORT STORIES

CONVERSATIONAL
DUTCH
DIALOGUES

Lingo Mastery

Conversational Dutch Dual Language Books Vol. 1

Is conversational Dutch turning a little too tricky for you? Do you have *no idea* how to order a meal or book a room at a hotel?

If your answer to any of the previous questions was *'Yes'*, then this book is for you!

If there's even been something tougher than learning the grammar rules of a new language, it's finding the way to speak with other people in that tongue. Any student knows this – we can try our best at practicing, but you always want to avoid making embarrassing mistakes or not getting your message through correctly.

'How do I get out of this situation?' many students ask themselves, to no avail, but no answer is forthcoming.

Until now.

We have compiled **MORE THAN ONE HUNDRED** conversational Dutch stories for beginners along with their translations, allowing new Dutch speakers to have the necessary tools to begin studying how to set a meeting, rent a car or tell a doctor that they don't feel well. We're not wasting time here with conversations that don't go anywhere: if you want to know how to solve problems (while learning a ton of Dutch along the way, obviously), this book is for you!

How Conversational Dutch Dialogues works:

- Each new chapter will have a fresh, new story between two people who wish to solve a common, day-to-day issue that you will surely encounter in real life.
- An Dutch version of the conversation will take place first, followed by an English translation. This ensures that you fully understood just what it was that they were saying.
- Before and after the main section of the book, we shall provide you with an introduction and conclusion that will offer you important strategies, tips and tricks to allow you to get the absolute most out of this learning material.
- That's about it! Simple, useful and incredibly helpful; you will **NOT** need another conversational Dutch book once you have begun reading and studying this one!

We want you to feel comfortable while learning the tongue; after all, no language should be a barrier for you to travel around the world and expand your social circles!

So look no further! Pick up your copy of **Conversational Dutch Dialogues** and start learning Dutch *right now*!

Made in United States
Orlando, FL
26 August 2022

21587817R00104